Contents

Welcome

1

Welcome!

Welcome to **PagePlus X7**, the award-winning Desktop Publishing (DTP) solution from Serif. PagePlus is the easiest way to get superior publishing results, whether on your desktop or via professional printing. It's simple for anyone to create, publish and share their designs as outstanding printed documents, stunning PDFs, PDF slideshows, tables/charts, modern eBooks or via web page.

To make life so much easier, PagePlus comes with an impressive selection of **design templates**, **creative content**, and **styles** for you to use. As a result, publishing to a professional standard is easily achievable for experienced and inexperienced users alike! You'll also be able to reuse existing content by importing PDF documents and word processing documents. On the flipside, you'll be able to export drawn objects to all the latest graphic file formats.

PagePlus X7 doesn't stop at superior publishing. Its range of design studios makes PagePlus stand out from the crowd—**Cutout Studio** for cutting pictures out from their backgrounds, **LogoStudio** for custom logo design, and **PhotoLab** for powerful image adjustment and effect combinations. You simply cannot afford to miss them!

Upgrading?

If you've upgraded from a previous version, this new edition of PagePlus includes a host of **exciting new features** which keeps PagePlus ahead of its competitors and at a fraction of the price! We hope you also enjoy the additional power and performance edge.

Registration

Don't forget to register your new copy, using the **Registration Wizard**, on the **Help** menu. That way, we can keep you informed of new developments and future upgrades!

New features

- **64-bit operation for improved performance**
  PagePlus is fully optimized for operation on 64-bit computers, and will automatically install for 64-bit operation accordingly.

- **Feed-based Startup Assistant** (see p. 13)
  The new-look starting point for new publications provides a wealth of constantly updating cross-product news and PagePlus-specific learning resources (video tutorials, written tutorials, help, and Tips & Tricks). The assistant keeps track of unread articles so you won't miss a thing! An Open option also gives you access to all your existing publications, based on document history.

- **Attractive eye-catching charts** (see p. 103)
  Present your **PagePlus table** in chart form using chart types including **Column**, **Bar**, **Line**, **Area**, **Pie**, and **Scatter Charts** (plus **3D** variants of each). Charts can be modified and chart **series** configured using the new **Charts** tab. For more chart design freedom, the **Chart Data** tab lets you manipulate standalone chart data (from scratch or derived from your PagePlus table) to your liking. Apply different chart "type - style" combinations in one click via the **Styles** tab.

Performance

- **Accelerated Graphics Technology**
  Performance and output quality are boosted by Serif's in-house processing technology—benefit from lighting fast drawing.

Ease of Use

- **Helpful guidance with Smart Hints**
  As you design your page, hints, warnings, tips, or general on-screen guidance appear on your page. You can control the number of Smart Hints displayed for both new and existing features.

- **Easy access to 2D/3D effects** (see p. 139)
  Shadows, glows, feathers, blurs, and more can be easily accessed on their own **Effects** tab. To complement these effects, a powerful collection of 3D effects are also available. Adjust individual settings for precise control or simply select preset gallery thumbnails.

- **More powerful tab control**
  PagePlus now offers more flexible docking options, including **Auto Hide** (to vertical sidebar), side-by-side docking, and nested grouping. **Docking indicator arrows** help you dock to top, bottom, left, or right of your workspace.

Colours

- **Print-focused CMYK primary colour mode**
  For native CMYK design-to-print colour management, PagePlus publications can now operate in CMYK primary colour mode.

- **Quick colour assignment with Colours toolbar** (see p. 149)
  The toolbar's **Fill**, **Line**, and **Text** buttons will remember the
  last applied solid, **gradient**, or **bitmap fill**. This makes light
  work of recolouring multiple objects.

- **Blend modes for creative page design** (see p. 164)
  For more adventurous colour experimentation, apply **blend
  modes** object-over-object for stunning results. Objects will also
  blend to coloured backgrounds (transparent by default).

- **Composite transparency and knockout groups**
  Assign transparency to a group using **composite transparency**!
  As another transparency control, **knockout groups** prevent
  overlapped, semi-transparent object areas from contributing
  their transparency to overlapping objects.

- **Composite blend modes and isolated blending** (see p. 164)
  Like composite transparency, a composite blend mode affects a
  group, after overlapping group objects are blended. For control
  of blending scope, **isolated blending** restricts blending effects
  to just the group (and not underlying objects).

- **Automatic gradient fill swatches** (see p. 154)
  PagePlus offers an **Automatic** fill category which hosts linear
  and radial swatches which are not based on fixed colours.
  Instead, the currently selected object's solid fill is used.

- **More gradient fills categories!** (see p. 154)
  The range of gradient fills available in PagePlus will be
  expanded to include **Radial**, **Plasma**, **Square**, **Three Colour**,
  and **Four Colour** fills.

Pictures

- **Repurpose vector images**
  Any metafile (SMF, WMF, EMF, or SVG) can be "broken apart" via **Tools>Convert To>Objects**. Vector objects can then be edited before optional re-exporting.

Tables

- **Flowing linked tables** (see p. 100)
  Like text frames, a single table can be physically split by row or column on the same page or over multiple pages. With the separated rows and columns remaining **linked**, added rows and columns will **reflow** within the table.

- **Presets for number formatting**
  For easier to use number formatting in table cells, the new **Number Formatting** dialog offers a selection of number format types to apply. Cell references using number formatting are more intuitive with no unnecessary formatting required.

Publishing and Exporting

- **Simpler PDF publishing** (see p. 178)
  A new and improved dialog offers only commonly used PDF settings via selectable profiles; advanced settings are stored under a collapsed **More Options** section if needed. PDF/X-3 compatibility is now provided via profile.

- **ePub export** (see p. 183)
  ePub export is compliant with the **epubcheck** compliance-checker tool, used by online services such as Apple iTunes and BookBaby.

- **New-look Export as Picture** (see p. 188)
  The improved **Export as Picture** feature **previews** your
  exported image, with **side-by-side comparisons** of different
  formats and **panning support**. **Export all pages** as separate
  pictures, **super sampling**, SVG export, and **export in greyscale**
  are all now possible.

and some enhancements on previous versions of PagePlus...

- The **Pages** tab lets you rearrange page order more easily via
  drag and drop. When moved, page thumbnails offer a
  suggested drop target.

- On PagePlus restart, optionally enable the **Restore Last Session**
  feature to reopen previously opened publications (view settings
  and current page display are preserved too!)

- Load a preset or custom workspace at any time from the Pages
  context toolbar.

- Assign **multiple master pages** simply by using **Ctrl**-drag.

- Convert as picture now offers all the power of the **Export as
  Picture** feature.

- **Recolour** picture options now include 'Recolour via HSL'
  and 'Recolour via LAB'.

Installation

Installing PagePlus follows different procedures depending on whether you are installing from disc or via download.

> 💡 You can install your new version alongside previous versions and use them independently.
>
> 💡 32 or 64-bit PagePlus X7 installs to respective 32 or 64-bit computers.

Installation procedure (from disc)

- Insert your purchased disc into your disc drive.

    - If AutoPlay is enabled on the drive, this automatically starts the Setup Wizard. Follow the on-screen instructions for install.

      -or-

    - If AutoPlay is not enabled (or doesn't start the install automatically), navigate to your program disc and double-click **autorun.exe**.

Installation procedure (from download)

- From **serif.com**, when logged into your Serif account, follow the on-screen instructions to download.

System Requirements

Minimum:

- Windows-based PC with DVD drive and mouse

- Operating systems:
  Microsoft Windows® XP SP3 (32 bit)
  Windows® Vista (32 or 64 bit)
  Windows® 7 (32 or 64 bit)
  Windows® 8 (32 or 64 bit)

- 512MB RAM (Windows® XP)
  1GB RAM (Windows® Vista and 32-bit Windows 7® and 8)
  2GB RAM (For 64-bit Windows® 7 and 8)

- 740MB free hard disk space

- 1024 x 768 monitor resolution (Use of Large Fonts may require a higher resolution)

Additional disk resources and memory are required when editing large and/or complex publications.

Optional:

- Windows-compatible printer

- TWAIN-compatible scanner and/or digital camera

- .NET 2.0 for text import filters (Word 2007/2010 + OpenOffice) (installed by default)

- Internet account and connection required for accessing online resources and .NET installation.

-

Getting Started

2

Startup Assistant

Once PagePlus has been installed, you're ready to start.

- For Windows Vista/7: Setup adds a **Serif PagePlus X7** item to the **All Programs** submenu of the Windows **Start** menu. Use the Windows **Start** button to pop up the Start menu, click on **All Programs** and then click **Serif PagePlus X7**.

- For Windows 8: The Setup routine during install adds a **Serif PagePlus** X7 entry to the desktop. Use the Windows **Start** button to pop up the desktop, and then click the PagePlus icon.

On program launch, the Startup Assistant is displayed which offers different routes into PagePlus.

The options are described as follows:

- The default home page keeps you in touch with Serif promotions and showcases articles (tutorials, etc.) You can also view the PagePlus Overview and Quick Start video

- **Open** - to access PagePlus publications, PDF files, or BookPlus files; also provides recent file history.

- **Learn** - for online video/written tutorials, help, tips & tricks, and more—all via a constantly updating feed that can be filtered by article Type. The Product Help and your PagePlus X7 user guide are also provided.

- **New Publication** - creates a new publication from scratch, based on a choice of page setups.

- **Templates** - creates a new publication based on one of many design templates.

- **News** - for cross-product news, company news, articles, and product announcements, using Serif's news feed.

 Any time you access the Startup Assistant, the Learn or News buttons indicate the number of new articles to be viewed (if available). This number will decrease as you read each article in the Learn or News pane.

When new articles arrive, these will be indicated the next time you open the Startup Assistant.

 Any new unread article arriving in the Learn or News pane will display a "new" indicator in its thumbnail.

Once you've clicked on a new article the "new" indicator changes to a "read" indicator.

Don't forget to use the keyword Search box at the top-right of the Startup Assistant. This is an incredibly powerful tool for filtering specific publication names, Learn articles, page sizes, theme layout names, or news articles.

To access the Startup Assistant when PagePlus is already running, choose **Startup Assistant** from the **File** menu.

Creating a publication from a design template

PagePlus comes complete with a whole range of categorized design templates which will speed you through the creation of all kinds of publications for desktop or commercial printing!

Each template offers:

- **Complementary design**—Professionally designed layout with high-visual impact.

- **Schemes**—choose a named colour scheme to apply a specific look and feel.

Design templates come in two types—**Theme Layouts**, where you pick your own pictures, or ready-to-go **Pro Templates** which are already populated with pictures.

Theme layouts offer a choice of themes (e.g., Ribbon) on which to base your publication (Brochure, Business Card, Flyer, Forms, Letterheads, Newsletter, etc.) ; you'll get picture placeholders instead of actual pictures. Simply add your own pictures to placeholders and personalize placeholder text, then publish.

You can also choose which page layouts you want to base your new publication on.

Ready-to-go Pro templates
These are categorized templates containing royalty-free photos which can be adopted to fast-track you to your completed publication. You just need to personalize placeholder text, then publish.

To create a publication from a design template:

1. Open PagePlus, or select **Startup Assistant** from the **File** menu.

2. Click **Templates**.

3. From the pane, select a Theme Layout or a design template from the Pro Template Packs category. Select from the tree menu in the left-hand pane.

Alternatively, simply choose a publication type from the same list, e.g. Brochures, Business Cards, etc. Scroll down the menu to display choices.

4. Navigate the main window's categories and sub-categories using the ⊕ **Expand** and ⊖ **Collapse** buttons, then click your chosen thumbnail.

Theme Layouts   *Pro Design Templates*

5. Examine the page sample(s) on the right. For theme layouts with multiple pages (e.g., brochures), you can choose which pages you wish to be part of your publication by checking the check box under each page. For design templates, simply review the pages to be part of your publication.

Theme Layouts   *Pro Design Templates*

6. Pick a **colour scheme** from the drop-down list at the top of the dialog. The page thumbnails refresh to reflect the new page's appearance.

	Scheme 01	▼
	Scheme 01	
	Scheme 02	
	Scheme 03	

7. Click **OK**. The pages are added to your new publication.

Starting a new publication from scratch

Although **design templates** can simplify your design choices, you can just as easily start out from scratch with a new, blank publication.

To start a new publication (via Startup Assistant):

1. Open PagePlus to display the **Startup Assistant**.
    - or -
    Select **Startup Assistant** from the **File** menu (during your session).

2. Select **New Publication**.

3. From the main pane, navigate the document categories by scrolling (click the ⊙ icon to expand if needed).

4. Click a publication thumbnail to create your new blank publication.

To create a publication using the default page type:

- During your PagePlus session, click  **New Publication** on the **Standard** toolbar.

To create a custom publication:

1. From the Startup Assistant's New Publication pane, click **Custom Publication**.

2. From the Publication Setup dialog, select a publication type, size, and orientation.

3. Click **OK**.

Opening existing publications

You can open a PagePlus publication from the **Startup Assistant**, **Standard** toolbar, or via the **File** menu.

It is also possible to open PDF files as new publications, or Import PDF files and existing PagePlus files into currently open publications. (See PagePlus Help for these import options.)

To open an existing publication (via Startup Assistant):

1. Open PagePlus to display the initial **Startup Assistant**.
   - or -
   Select **Startup Assistant** from the **File** menu (during your session).

2.   Select **Open**.

3.   Several options are possible:

i.   For recently opened publications, select a thumbnail from the main pane.

Filter Document History ▼

Today

Charts - Sample

ii.   The publication opens in your workspace.

- or -

i.   For other PagePlus publications, PDF files, or BookPlus files, select from the Browse My Computer pane.

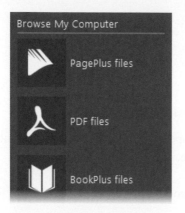

ii.   From the dialog, locate and select your file, then click
Open.

To open existing publications (without Startup Assistant):

- Click **Open** on the **Standard** toolbar.

Saving your publication

To save your work:

1. Click **Save** on the **Standard** toolbar.

2. To save under a different name, choose **Save As** from the **File**
   menu.

> Unsaved publications have an asterisk after their name in the
> PagePlus title bar, **Publications** toolbar, and **Window** menu.

Pages

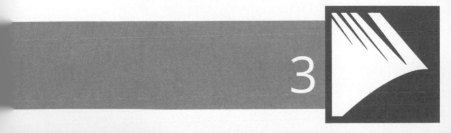

3

Setting up a publication

A publication's **page size** and **orientation** settings are fundamental to your layout, and are defined when the new publication is first created, either **using a design template** or as a **new publication**.

To adjust size/orientation of the current publication:

1. Select ▥ **Publication Setup** from the Pages context toolbar.

2. Ensure the **Paper** menu option is selected. The other option, **Margins**, lets you define non-printable Margin, Row, Column, and Bleed Guides as design aids.

3. For a **Regular/Booklet Publication**, you can select a pre-defined paper size, printer-derived paper size, or enter custom values for page **Width** and **Height**, as well as setting the orientation (Portrait or Landscape). For booklets only, select a type from the **Booklet** drop-down list, which page to start on (left/right), and if you require **Facing pages** (including **Dual master pages**). PagePlus automatically performs **imposition**.

4. For other publication types, you can select: **Small Publications** (for example, business cards, labels, etc.), **Large Publications** (posters), or **Folded Publications** (cards).

    -   For Small publications, enable **Paper** and choose a pre-defined option from the list, or for creating **Labels**, enable the radio button and pick an Avery label code which matches your labels.

    -   For Large and Folded publications, choose a pre-defined option from the list (use the preview).

5. Click **OK** to accept the new dimensions. The updated settings will be applied to the current publication.

Once you've set up your publication, you can optionally include repeated page elements on every page by creating **master pages** (p. 28).

Uniform and mixed page orientations

If you've changed your mind about the page orientation chosen at page setup, you can change the page orientation uniformly across your publication at any time.

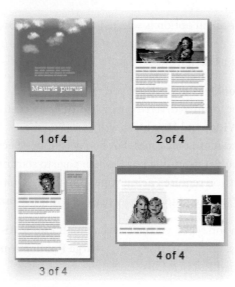

To change all publication pages from portrait to landscape (or vice versa):

- On the Pages context toolbar, click the down arrow on the **Publication Orientation** button, then select **Landscape Publication** (or **Portrait Publication**) from the flyout.

To change a page from portrait to landscape (or vice versa):

1. On the Pages tab, double-click to select a page.

2. Click **Change page orientation** to swap between portrait and landscape orientation.

- or -

From the Pages context toolbar, click the down arrow on the **Page orientation** button, then select **Landscape Page** (or **Portrait Page**) from the flyout.

You can repeat the procedure for any other selected page.

This feature is only applicable for publications using standard page sizes (e.g., A4, A5, Letter, etc.)

Imposition

For press-ready output, you have the option to use **imposition** at the PDF or print stage, allowing you to create a folded publication (e.g., booklet or greeting card) from a non-folding publication without having to choose a folding publication in advance.

Adding, removing, and rearranging pages

Use the **Pages tab** to add/delete standard or **master pages**, **assign master pages** to standard pages, and rearrange standard pages using drag-and-drop. You can also change **page orientations**.

To add a single page:

1. On the **Pages** tab, click once to select a page in the **Pages** window. The thumbnail that's shown as "selected" is independent of the page you're currently working on. To work on a particular page, double-click its thumbnail.

2. Click [icon] **Add** to add a page (or master page) *before* the one selected in the window.
   - or -
   To add a new page *at the end* of the publication, deselect all pages by clicking in the neutral region of the lower window, then click the **Add** button.

To add master pages:

For **master pages**, the above procedure applies but you need to click **Master Pages** to open its window first.

To delete a single page/master page:

1. On the **Pages** tab, select the page (or master page) to delete on the appropriate window by clicking its thumbnail.

2. Click 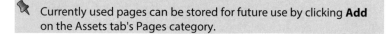 **Remove**.

To rearrange pages:

- On the **Pages** tab, in the lower **Pages** window, drag a page thumbnail over another page thumbnail in the page sequence. The page is added after the hovered over page thumbnail.

Adding more template pages

Use the Assets tab's Asset Browser if you're looking to use some additional template pages in your publication. See **Browsing** on p. 45.

You can drag-and-drop a page to replace (or add before/after) your current page.

> Currently used pages can be stored for future use by clicking **Add** on the Assets tab's Pages category.

Understanding master pages

Master pages provide a flexible way to store background elements that you'd like to appear on more than one page—for example a logo, background, header/footer, or border design.

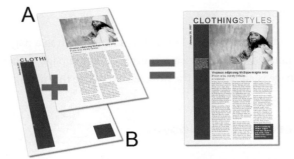

*(**A**) Page, (**B**) Master Page*

The key concept here is that a particular master page is typically **shared** by multiple pages, as illustrated below. By placing a design element on a master page and then assigning several pages to use that master page, you ensure that all the pages incorporate that element. Of course, each individual page can have its own "foreground" elements.

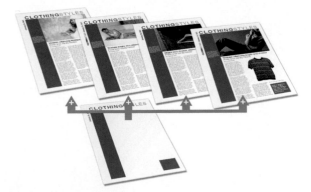

Master pages are available in every publication, but in a simple publication you may not need to use any master pages—or you may need only one master page. Facing pages and multiple master pages prove valuable with longer, more complex publications.

> If you're starting with a design template you may encounter one or more master pages incorporated with the design.

Using the **Pages** tab or **Page Manager**, you can quickly add or delete master pages; for example, you could set up different master pages for "title" or "chapter divider" pages.

Assigning master pages

If you're only using one master page it is assigned to any newly created page by default. However, if you're using multiple master pages you can assign a different master page to a standard page, all, odd or even pages. It's even possible to assign multiple master pages per page.

> You'll need to create an additional master page first. See **Adding, removing, and rearranging pages** on p. 28.

> Each new page or master page consists of a single **layer**; a page with a master page also shows the master page's Master Layer.

To assign a master page:

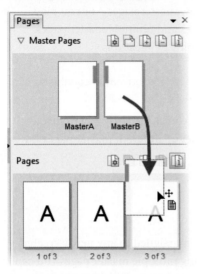

- From the expanded Master Pages window in the Pages tab, drag a master page onto a target standard page in the lower window.

Click **Page Identifiers** to indicate the master pages used on the currently selected page(s). The master page is represented as a letter on the Page, e.g. A, B, C, etc.

Assigning multiple master pages

Just like a regular page, the master page can have its own set of **layers** associated with it, completely unique from the regular page! For a single master page assigned to a page, on the Layers tab, you'll see a master layer (e.g., 'Master Layer 1 [A]') as a separate entry. However, you can assign additional master pages to your page for more powerful page design.

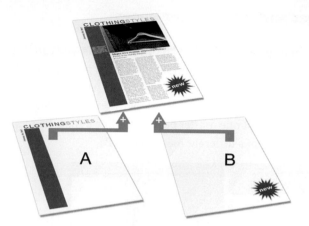

In the example above, a newly assigned master page B would add a new master layer ('Master Layer 2 [B]') to the publication page's Layers tab.

For an introduction to the concept of layers, see **Working with layers** on p. 38.

> An additional master page needs to be created first. See **Adding, removing, and rearranging pages** on p. 28.

To assign multiple master pages to a page:

- On the **Pages** tab, **Ctrl**-drag a master page thumbnail from the Master Page window onto the chosen page's thumbnail in the Pages window.

To jump to a master page from the selected publication page:

- Double-click on a Master Layer entry in the Layers tab.

The master page assigned to the master layer is displayed.

Facing pages and dual master pages

If you're using multi-page **regular/booklet publications**, you can assign different master pages to the left and right publication pages (also called spreads) if necessary—master pages are assigned per page and not per spread. For example (see below), a left-hand "body text" page might use the left-side component of one master page (**A**), while a right-hand page could use the right side of a different master page (**B**).

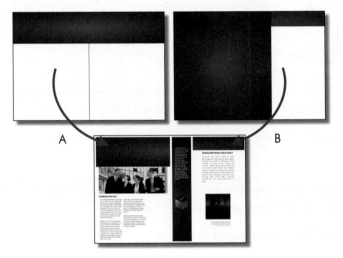

A   B

Editing master page objects

If you're editing pages which use master pages, master page objects will contribute to your page design. These objects can be edited quickly and easily from the page by using a control bar under the selected object.

- Click ✛A **Edit on Master Page** to jump to the master page and edit the object there.

- Click ⚓A **Promote from Master Page** to disconnect the object from the master page and make it independently editable on the publication page.

Using page numbering

Page number fields automatically display the current page number. Typically, these fields are added automatically to the **master page** (so they appear on every page) with the Header and Footers Wizard (**Insert** menu), but you can insert a page number field anywhere in your master page text.

You can change the style of page numbers, create mixed page number formats, set starting page number(s), and control number continuation across chapters and publication sections (all via **Page Number Format** on the **Format** menu).

To insert a page number field:

1. Switch to the master page (if desired) by clicking 🄰1 **View Master Pages** on the Hintline.

2. With the **Artistic Text Tool** selected (**Tools** toolbar), click for an insertion point to place the page number.

3. On the **Insert** menu, select **Page Number** from the **Information** flyout.

You can also specify the **First Page Number** in the sequence (this will appear on the first page of the publication). For example, Chapter Two of a long publication might be in a separate file and begin numbering with page 33.

To set the first page number:

1. Uncheck **Continue from previous chapter**. PagePlus keeps this checked by default so that number continuation is maintained if your publication is to be part of a book.

2. Enter a different **First Page Number**.

For simple publications, it's likely that the same page format is used (e.g., Arabic numerals throughout). However, for more complex publications, different formats can be used for different page ranges, with each page range belonging to its own **publication section**. See PagePlus Help.

Navigating pages

To switch between pages:

- ◀ ▶ ▮◀ ▶▮ On the **Hintline**, click **Previous Page**, **Next Page**, **First Page** or **Last Page**.

  - or -

  Click in the **Current Page** box (e.g., 2 of 4) and type the page number you want to jump to.

  - or -

  On the **Pages** tab, double-click the page's thumbnail for the page (or master page) you want to view.

To switch between current page and its master page:

- From the **Hintline**, click ▣ **Master Pages**.

Viewing pages

Most of the PagePlus display is taken up by a page or "artwork" area and a surrounding "pasteboard" area.

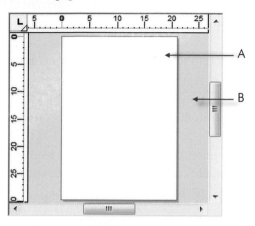

In PagePlus, the **Page** area (**A**) is where you add and position your text, shapes, and pictures that you want to print. The **Pasteboard** area (**B**) is where you generally keep any text, shapes, or pictures that are being prepared or waiting to be positioned on the page area. Drag objects from pasteboard to target page when ready.

PagePlus makes it easy to see exactly what you're working on—from a wide view of multiple pages to a close-up view of a small region. For example, you can use the **scroll bars** at the right and bottom of the main window to move the page and pasteboard with respect to the main window. If you're using a **wheel mouse**, you can scroll vertically by rotating the wheel, or horizontally by **Shift**-scrolling. You can also pan around the page by clicking the mouse wheel down and dragging.

Magnifying pages

For magnification options, the **Hintline** toolbar provides the:

Zoom to Current option to zoom to a selected object, or to the page width if no objects are selected.

Zoom Tool to zoom into an area defined by a drawn marquee selection.

Pan Tool for moving around the zoomed-in page by dragging.

165% **Current Zoom** option to display or change the level of magnification. To change, click to select from a flyout or enter a custom percentage value directly.

⊖ **Zoom Out** and ⊕ **Zoom In** tools so you can inspect and/or edit the page at different levels of detail. Alternatively, use the Zoom slider to alter the zoom level instead these buttons.

Working with layers

When you create a new publication from scratch or from some design templates, the page(s) you create will initially consist of two **layers**—one for the page (Layer 1) and one for the associated **master page** (see p. 30). The layers can be seen within a hierarchical stack on the **Layers tab**.

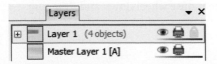

One layer may be enough to accommodate the elements of a particular layout, but you can create additional layers as needed for the page.

Multiple layers are useful for complex designs as you can concentrate on one layer at a time without affecting objects on other layers.

A useful feature of the Layers tab is that you can see objects under the layer on which they were created. By expanding the layer by clicking ⊞ , these objects are displayed—with a click, they can be **selected** on the page.

The above layer stack could represent the following:

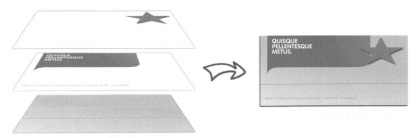

Master Layer, Layer 1, and Layer 2 from bottom to top.

Cumulative layers as seen on the page.

To select a particular layer:

- Click a layer name. The layer entry shows a blue background.

To display master page layers:

- Double-click the master layer entry. The Layers tab now shows the master page's layers and the master page is shown in the workspace. See **Understanding master pages** on p. 30.

Adding, removing, and rearranging layers

Once you've created a page, it's easy to add, delete, and move layers.

To add a new layer to the current page or master page:

1. In the Layers tab, click ⬧ **Add Layer**.

2. You'll be prompted to give the new layer a name and set its **properties**. When you've made your selections, click **OK**.

The new layer is inserted above the currently selected layer. If a layer is not selected, the new layer is placed at the top of the stack.

To delete a layer:

- In the Layers tab, select the layer's name and click ▭ **Delete Selected Layers**.

To move a layer:

- In the Layers tab, drag a layer entry to a new position in the layer stack.

To set layer properties on the tab:

- Click the 👁 icon to hide/show the layer and any objects on it.

- Click the 🖶 icon to exclude/include the layer in printouts.

- Click the 🔒 icon to prevent/allow objects on the layer from being selected/edited.

Assets for Creativity

4

Using assets

An **asset** is a general term for any object or page element that can be added to your page to enhance its appearance, increase efficiency, or personalize your design. Assets range from graphics, logos, **pictures**, picture **frames**, and backgrounds (as shown below) to more complex page content and entire pages.

To use assets, PagePlus provides the **Assets tab**, powered by both an **Asset Browser** (p. 45) and Asset Manager (see PagePlus Help). The former browses your assets stored within installed Asset Packs, the latter lets you create and manage custom Asset Packs.

> ✎ **Theme Layout** design templates come complete with their own built-in assets, all themed to the publication's design. When you start from a theme layout the Assets tab will be populated with associated assets automatically!

Using the Assets tab

The **Assets tab** is a powerful design resource that exclusively hosts your browsed assets, ready for adding to your publication page.

Assets can be placed into the following categories.

- **My Designs**: Stores custom assets dragged from the page.

- **Graphics**: Stores professional clipart from Asset Packs.

- **Pictures**: Stores added pictures from your hard disk (or from Asset Pack, if containing pictures).

- **Picture Frames**: Stores picture frames from Asset Packs.

- **Page Content**: Stores page content (pre-assembled from various page objects) from Asset Packs.

- **Backgrounds**: Stores backgrounds from Asset Packs.

- **Pages**: Stores complete ready-to-go pages from Asset Packs.

The tab also lets you create custom designs for reuse globally or just in your publication. You'll be able to:

- Store your own designs to the tab's My Designs category for global use.

- Store your own designs to any other tab's category for current publication use.

- Create custom **picture frames** from drawn shapes.

- Create page backgrounds from pictures/filled page objects.

- Create custom page content (combinations of assets).

Although initially empty, the tab can be populated with assets of your choice by using an Asset Browser.

The Asset Browser

The Asset Browser lets you browse by asset category and Asset Pack (Pack Files), as well as search (by tag) for assets. Once displayed, the asset can be selected for inclusion in the Assets tab.

The Asset Manager

Use the **Asset Manager** to create your own Asset Packs by using assets from other Asset Packs and/or by importing pictures, graphics, or backgrounds. You can tag assets and then save your custom asset pack.

Browsing

The **Asset Browser** offers professional ready-to-go designs that you can use directly in your publication. These designs are provided in categorized Asset Packs installed with PagePlus. You can browse these packs and preview their contents, before adding assets to your workspace.

To browse assets (by category):

1. From the Assets tab, click **Browse**.

2. In the **Asset Browser**, select an asset category from the **Categories** section. You'll see installed Asset Packs appear in the main pane, stored under their Pack file names, e.g. Arctic.

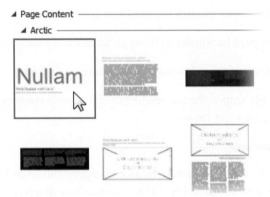

3. Scroll through the asset packs to browse assets in each pack.

To browse assets (by Asset Pack):

1. From the Assets tab, click **Browse**.

2. In the **Asset Browser**, on the left-hand side of the dialog, select an asset pack name from the **Pack Files** section, e.g., Backgrounds. The Asset Pack will appear in the main pane.

3. The assets are categorized further in the main pane by the name of the Asset Pack to which they belong, e.g., Fun. Scroll through to browse the assets included in each Asset Pack.

Searching for assets

The search facility filters assets based on preset and custom tags applied to all of the Asset Packs shown in the **Asset Browser**.

To apply a search filter:

- For a simple tag search, type the word or letter you want to search for in the **Search** text box, situated at the top right of the dialog. This is useful for retrieving assets with custom tags attached.

Search	🔍

business	✕

Filtering assets

Filtering means that you can restrict the amount of assets on display.

- For **category** and/or **pack file filtering**, select a category or pack file (or multiple instances using **Ctrl**-click). You can also search for category and pack file combinations.

mart Tags
- Agriculture
- Clipart
- Colours
- Education
- Geography
- Food & Drink
- Drink
- Food
- History
- Landmarks & Buildings

- For **Smart tag filtering**, select a tag name from the **Smart Tags** section. Smart tags let you filter assets logically by subject matter using a hierarchical and alphabetic tag structure.

- For **single-tag filtering**, select a tag name from the **Tags** section of the Asset Browser. (You may need to scroll down the left-hand pane to view). Use **Ctrl**-click to manually select multiple tags.

Adding assets to your Assets tab

To add a specific asset:

- Select the **category** or **pack file** in the Asset Browser, and then simply click the asset. A check mark shows on the thumbnail.

To add all assets:

- Click **Add All**  from the upper-right corner of each Asset Pack's thumbnail gallery. Check marks will show on all thumbnails.

With either method, asset(s) will be available to you from the Assets tab when you close the Asset Browser.

> Any asset stored in your Assets tab (but not added to the page) will be available to you the next time you open your publication. Assets can be made globally available by usings the pins (and) in the relevant tab category. Custom designs can also be made global by dragging page objects to the tab's My Designs category.

Adding assets to your page

To add an asset to the page:

- Click an asset's thumbnail in your chosen category and drag it onto the page.

Manipulating Objects

Selecting an object

Before you can change any object, you need to select it using one of a choice of tools on the **Tools** toolbar.

 Pointer Tool

Click to use the **Pointer Tool** to select, move, copy, resize or rotate objects.

 Lasso Tool

Click to use the **Lasso Tool** to draw a freeform region under which any objects will become selected.

To select an object:

- Click on the "glowing" hovered over object using one of the tools shown above, to reveal a bounding box around the object.

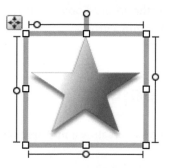

If objects overlap, use the **Alt** key while clicking repeatedly until the desired object is selected.

For precise object selection in more complex page designs, use the **Lasso Tool** on the **Tools** toolbar.

To select a text object with the Pointer Tool:

- Clicking on a text object (artistic text or text frame) with the Pointer Tool selects the object and also positions the blinking text selection cursor within the object's text. In this mode, you can **edit the text** (see p. 82).

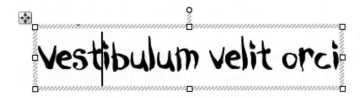

- Double-, triple-, or quadruple-click to select a word, paragraph, or all text.

- To select only the text frame, click the frame's bounding box.

- Clicking on a **group** selects the grouped object. **Ctrl**-click to select an individual object within a group.

Selecting multiple objects

Selecting more than one object at a time (creating a **multiple selection**) lets you:

- Position or resize all the objects at the same time.

- Create a **group object** from the multiple selection, which can then be treated as a single object, with the option of restoring the individual objects later. See **Creating groups** on p. 53.

To create a multiple selection:

- Drag a "marquee" box around the objects you want to select.

Alternatively, either hold down the **Shift** key and click each object in turn.

To add or remove an object from a multiple selection:

- Hold down the **Shift** key and click the object to be added or removed.

To deselect all objects in a multiple selection:

- Click in a blank area of the page.

Creating groups

You can easily turn a **multiple selection** into a group object. When objects are grouped, you can **position**, **resize**, or **rotate** the objects all at the same time.

To create a group from a multiple selection:

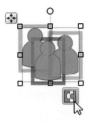

- Click the **Group Objects** button.

To ungroup:

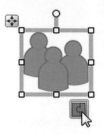

- Click the **Ungroup Objects** button. The group turns back to a multiple selection.

To select an individual object within a group:

- **Ctrl**-click the object.

Copying, pasting, and duplicating objects

Besides using the Windows Clipboard to copy and paste objects, you can duplicate objects easily using drag-and-drop.

To copy an object (or multiple selection) to the Windows Clipboard:

- Click **Copy** on the **Standard** toolbar.

If you're using another Windows application, you can usually copy and paste objects via the Clipboard.

To paste an object from the Clipboard:

- Click **Paste** on the **Standard** toolbar.

The standard Paste command inserts the object at the insertion point or (for a separate object) at the centre of the page.

To duplicate an object:

1. Select the object, then press the **Ctrl** key.

2. Drag the object via the 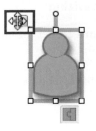 **Move** button to a new location on the page, then release the mouse button.

Moving objects

To move an object (including a multiple selection):

-   Drag the selected object(s) by using its **Move** button. Once you see a move cursor over the button you can begin dragging.

Resizing objects

PagePlus provides several methods for resizing single or grouped objects.

To resize an object:

1. Select the object.

2. Click one of the selection handles and drag inwards or outwards.

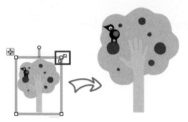

Dragging from an edge handle resizes in one dimension, by moving that edge. Dragging from a corner handle resizes in two dimensions, by moving two edges.

To resize freely:

- Drag from a corner (or line end) handle.

To constrain an object's dimensions when resizing:

- Hold the **Shift** key down and drag from a corner (or line end) handle.

For shapes, this has the effect of keeping a square as a square, a circle as a circle, etc.

 For pictures, dimensions are constrained on dragging a corner handle. Use **Shift**-drag to resize a picture freely.

For pictures, dimensions are constrained on dragging a corner handle. Use **Shift**-drag to resize a picture freely.

To resize about the object centre instead, press the **Ctrl** key as you drag edge or corner handles; **Ctrl**+**Shift**+drag to for a constrained resize about the object centre.

You can also make fine resizing adjustments from the Transform tab.

Ordering objects

On each layer, objects such as text frames, graphics, and pictures are **stacked** in the order you create them, from back to front, with each new object in front of the others.

For example, the left-most beige button above can be brought from the back to the front of the object order.

To shift the selected object's position to the bottom or top of the stack:

- Click **Send to Back** or **Bring to Front** on the **Arrange** toolbar, respectively.

To shift the object's position one step toward the back or front:

- Click **Back One** or **Forward One** on the **Arrange** toolbar, respectively.

Aligning and distributing objects

Aligning and distributing objects gives your project a professional feel. With PagePlus, you can align your objects in relation to each other or the page using dynamic guides or the **Align** tab.

Aligning with dynamic guides

As you draw, you can align any moving object with fixed objects on the page using dynamic guides. By default, these red-coloured guides only show as you move objects, suggesting possible objects that can aligned and snapped to.

For example, a moving yellow square can be aligned to the left edge of a fixed blue square.

Aligning with the Align tab

Alignment involves taking a group of selected objects and aligning them all in one operation by their top, bottom, left or right edges. You can also distribute objects, so that your objects (as a multiple selection) are spread evenly (optionally at spaced intervals).

To align the edges of two or more objects in a selection:

1. Using the Pointer Tool, **Shift**-click on all the objects you want to align, or draw a marquee box around them, to create a multiple selection.

2. Select the **Align** tab.

3.   Select an option for vertical and/or horizontal alignment.
     Choose **Top**, **Bottom**, **Left**, **Right**, **Centre Horizontally** or
     Centre Vertically, i.e.

To distribute two or more objects across a selection:

- Choose  **Space Evenly Across** or **Space Evenly Down**
  to spread selected objects uniformly between endmost objects
  in the current selection (horizontally or vertically, respectively)
  or by a set measurement (choose **Spaced** and set a value in any
  measurement unit).

Rather than work within the current selection area you can align or
distribute to page margins (if set), page/spread edge, or last selected
object.

To align/distribute objects to page margins, edges, or across
page spreads:

Relative to: Selection ▼

Selection
Last Selected
Margins
Page
Spread

- Select from the **Relative to**
  drop-down list to align the
  selected object(s) within the
  page **Margins**, **Page** edges, or
  Spread (for facing pages) then
  choose an align or distribute
  button described above.

For more advanced alignment control, you can align multiple objects in
relation to your last selected object (select objects in turn with the **Shift**
key pressed) by using the **Relative to: Last Selected** drop-down list
option. The last selected object is shown with a darker bounding box
when compared to other selected objects.

> For marquee selection, the lower-most object in the Z-order, i.e. on
> the object's layer, is considered the last selected.

Rotating an object

You can rotate single and multiple objects, including pictures, text objects, and groups using the object's rotation handle.

To rotate a selected object (using its rotation handle):

- Click and drag the rotation handle extending from the selection box (use the **Shift** key while dragging for 15° rotation intervals).

To undo rotation (then restore the original orientation):

- Double-click the object's rotation handle.

- To restore the rotated position, double-click the rotation handle again.

To change the rotation origin:

1. Click the object's rotation handle.

2. Move the rotation origin ⊕ away from its original position in the centre of the object to any position on the object or page (ideal for rotating grouped objects around a central point).

3. Drag the rotation handle to a new rotation angle—the object will rotate about the new origin.

To reset the rotation origin, simply double-click it.

To rotate an object 90 degrees left or right:

- Select the object and click  **Rotate Left** or **Rotate Right** on the **Arrange** toolbar.

Anchoring objects to text

If you're working with text frames you'll probably want to add supporting shapes, pictures, tables, or even nested text frames within your publication's text (artistic or frame text). Such objects can be positioned either in relation to a position in your text (or other page element) or be simply placed inline in your text. In either instance, objects can then move with the text as you add further text content.

In PagePlus, this positioning is controlled by **anchoring** an object.

- **Float with text**. The object is positioned horizontally and vertically relative to an ⚓ **anchor point**. This option is ideal for pictures, pulled quotes, etc.

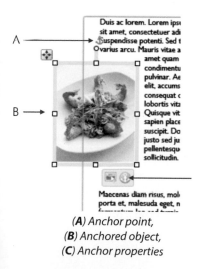

(A) Anchor point,
(B) Anchored object,
(C) Anchor properties

Pasted text (red box) causes reflow

- **Position inline as character**. The anchored object is placed as a character in the text and aligned in relation to the text that surrounds it. The anchored object flows with the text as before.

- **Detach from text**. The anchored object is disconnected from its anchor point, leaving a normal unanchored object.

PagePlus objects can be anchored to anywhere in your publication text, but the floated object can be positioned in relation to indented text, column, frame, page margin guides, the page itself, or most typically the anchor point in a text frame.

For text frames, when the text reflows, the anchor point (and therefore anchored object) reflows with the text. This allows supporting anchored objects to always stay with supporting text as more text is added to the frame.

To create an anchored object:

1. Position your unanchored object on the page.

2. Select **Anchor Object** from the **Arrange** menu.

3. From the dialog, choose a positioning option:

Either, for a **floating** object:

i. Enable **Float with text**. This is the default positioning option.

ii. Click **OK**. The ⚓ **Anchor point** appears and your object is now an anchored (showing an 🔘 icon).

Or, for an **inline** object:

    i.   Enable **Position inline as character**.

    ii.   Click **OK**. The object appears inline with text, and shows an 🔵 **Anchor Properties** icon.

> ⚲ Frame text can wrap around floating anchored objects (see **Wrapping text**; p. 91).

To view anchor properties:

1.   Select an anchored object.

2.   Click ⚓ **Anchored Object Properties** shown under the object.

To disconnect an anchored object:

- Enable **Detach from text**.

Updating and saving defaults

Object defaults are the stored property settings PagePlus applies to newly created objects such as:

- **lines** and **shapes** (line and fill colour, shade, pattern, transparency, etc.)

- **frames** (margins, columns, etc.)

- **text** (i.e., font, size, colour, alignment, etc.). Defaults are saved separately for **artistic, shape**, **frame** and **table text.**

Default settings are always **local**—that is, any changed defaults apply to the current publication and are automatically saved with it, so they're in effect next time you open that publication.

You can use the **Save Defaults** command to record the current defaults as **global** settings that will be in effect for any new publication you subsequently create.

To set local defaults for a particular type of object:

1.   Create a single sample object and fine-tune its properties as desired—or use an existing object that already has the right properties.

2.   Select the object that's the basis for the new defaults and from the **Format** menu, select **Update Object Default**.

Or, for line and fill colours, including line styles:

1.   With no object selected, choose the required line and/or fill colours from the Colour or Swatches tab. Use the Line tab to set a default line weight, style, and corner shape.

2.   Draw your object on the page, which will automatically adopt the newly defined default colours and styles.

To view and change default text properties:

1.   From the **Format** menu, select **Text Style Palette**.

2.   Double-click **Default Text**, then from the expanded list of text types, choose an option (e.g., Artistic Text).

3.   Click **Modify** to view current settings for the selected text type.

4.   Use the Text Style dialog to alter character, paragraph, or other properties.

To save all current defaults as global settings:

1.   From the **Tools** menu, select **Save Default Settings**.

2.   From the dialog, check options to update specific defaults.

3.   Click **Save** to confirm that you want new publications to use the checked object's defaults globally.

Text

Understanding text frames

Typically, text in PagePlus goes into **text frames**, which work equally
well as containers for single words, standalone paragraphs, multipage
articles, or chapter text.

> You can also use **artistic text** (see p. 78) for standalone text with
> special effects, or **table text** (on p. 99) for row-and-column displays.

What's a text frame?

A text frame is a container (like a mini-page) in which the main text for
your publication is stored; in PagePlus, the frame text in the frame is
actually called a **story**.

Lorem ipsum dolor sit amet, consectetuer adipiscing elit. Cras gravida
sem ut massa. Quisque accumsan porttitor dui. Sed interdum, nisl ut
consequat tristique, lacus nulla porta massa, sed imperdiet sem nunc
vitae eros. Vestibulum ante ipsum primis in faucibus orci luctus.

The text frame can be sized and positioned in advance of, or after adding
body text. When you move a text frame, its **story text** moves with it.
When you resize a text frame, its story text reflows to the new
dimensions.

Perhaps the most important feature of text frames is the ability to flow
text between linked text frames on the same or different pages. See
Fitting text to frames on p. 74.

For now we'll look at a text frame as an object and the frame text
contained within a single frame.

Frame linking

Frames can be linked so that a single story continues from one frame to another. But text frames can just as easily stand alone. Thus in any publication, you can create text in a single frame, spread a story over several frames, and/or include completely independent frames. By placing text frames anywhere, in any order, you can build up newspaper or newsletter style publications with a story flowing:

- between linked frames on the same page.

Vestibulum semper enim non eros. Sed vitae arcu. Aliquam erat volutpat. Praesent odio nisl, suscipit at, rhoncus sit amet, porttitor sit amet, leo. Aenean hendrerit est. Etiam ac augue. Morbi tincidunt neque ut lacus. Duis vulputate cursus orci. Mauris justo lorem, scelerisque sit amet, placerat sed, condimentum in, leo. Donec urna est, semper quis, auctor eget, ultrices in, purus. Etiam rutrum. Aliquam blandit dui a libero.

- between linked frames on different pages.

cidunt neque ut lacus. Duis vulputate scelerisque sit amet, placerat sed, semper quis, auctor eget, ultrices in, di a libero. Praesent tortor tortor, bib

quis nibh

eros. Sed vitae arcu. Aliquam erat volutpat pit at, rhoncus sit amet, porttitor sit amet, leo. am ac augue. Morbi tincidunt neque ut lacus. Duis uris justo lorem, scelerisque sit amet, placerat sed, nec urna est, semper quis, auctor eget, ultrices in, purus. Etiam rutrum. Aliquam blandit dui a libero. Praesent tortor tortor, bib

- from one column to another in the same frame.

In eget sapien vitae massa rhoncus lacinia. Nullam at leo neo metus aliquam semper. Phasellus tincidunt, ante nec lacinia ultrices quam mi dictum libero, bibendum turpis elit ut lectus. Sed diam ante, lobortis sed, dignissim sit amet, condimentum in, sapien. Pellentesque nec lectus non risus auctor lobortis. Vestibulum sit amet dolor a ante suscipit pulvinar. Sed lacinia. Aliquam erat volutpat. In hac habitasse platea dictumst. Vivamus sit amet sem vitae tellus ultricies consequat. Integer tincidunt tellus eget justo. Class aptent taciti sociosqu ad litora torquent per conubia nostra, per inceptos hymenaeos. Vivamus vel sapien. Praesent nisl tortor, laoreet eu, dapibus quis, egestas non, mauris. Cum sociis natoque penatibus et magnis dis parturient montes, nascetur ridiculus mus. Nullam eleifend pharetra felis. Mauris nibh velit, tristique ac, lacinia in, scelerisque et, ante. Donec viverra tortor sed nulla. Phasellus nec magna. Aenean vehicula, turpis in congue eleifend, mauris lorem aliquam sem, eu eleifend est odio et pede.

Creating text frames

You add text frames and position them on the page as you would any other object, in advance of adding text content.

To create a frame:

1. Select **Standard Text Frame** on the **Tools** toolbar.

2. Click on the page or pasteboard to create a new frame at a default size.
   - or -
   Drag out to place the text frame at your chosen dimensions.

To delete a frame:

- Select the frame—click its edge until a solid border appears— and then press the **Delete** key.

You can **select**, **move**, and **resize** text frames just like other objects (see p. 51, 55, and 55, respectively). When you select a frame's bounding box, indicated by a solid border, you can manage the frame properties; selecting inside a frame creates a blinking insertion point in the frame's text (the frame's boundary box becomes hatched to indicate editing mode). In this mode, you can edit the text. (For details, see **Editing text on the page** on p. 82.)

PagePlus also lets you create a wide variety of shaped frames from closed shapes or **QuickShapes** (see p. 132).

To create a frame (from a shape):

1. Draw a shape with a **line tool** or create a QuickShape.

2. Select **Convert To>Shaped Text Frame** from the **Tools** menu (or use object's right-click menu).
   - or -

   Type directly onto the QuickShape to automatically create a shaped frame.

Putting text into a frame

You can put text into a frame using one of the following methods:

WritePlus story editor:	With a selected frame, click **Edit story in WritePlus** on the Frame context toolbar.
Importing text:	Select the frame, then select **Text File** from the **Insert** menu.
Typing into the frame:	Select the Pointer Tool, then click for an insertion point to type text straight into a frame, or edit existing text. (See **Editing text on the page** on p. 82.)

Pasting via the Clipboard: At an insertion point in the text, press **Ctrl+V**.

Drag and drop: Select text (e.g. in a word processor file), then drag it onto the PagePlus page.

Adding pictures into a text frame

Pictures can be placed inline at any point in your story in a text frame, with PagePlus prompting you to resize the picture to fit with the text frames dimensions if it is too large.

If you add further story text before the picture, the inline picture will move with the surrounding text.

To add a picture to a text frame:

1. Add an empty paragraph to your text frame at the point you want to add your picture, i.e. press Return at the end of an existing paragraph.

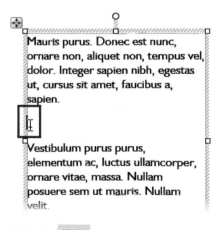

2. From the **Picture** flyout on the **Tools** toolbar, click **Import Picture**.

3. Navigate to your picture, select it and click **Open**.

4. If the picture dimensions exceed those of the text frame, click **Yes** in the displayed dialog to scale down the picture.

Frame setup and layout

The **frame layout** controls how text will flow in the frame. The frame can contain multiple **columns**. When a frame is selected, its column margins appear as dashed grey guide lines if set in **Frame Setup**. Note that unlike the page margin and row/column guides, which serve as layout guides for placing page elements, the frame column guides actually determine how text flows within each frame. Text won't flow outside the column margins.

You can drag the column guides or use a dialog to adjust the top and bottom **column blinds** and the left and right **column margins**.

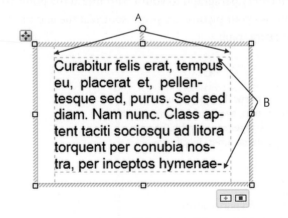

(**A**) *Column margins*, (**B**) *Column blinds*.

To edit frame properties directly:

- Select the frame object, then drag column guide lines to adjust the boundaries of the column.

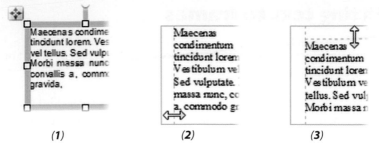

(1)   *(2)*   *(3)*

The frame edge is clicked to show a **selected** bounding box (**1**), after dragging inwards the column margin can be adjusted (**2**), and after dragging downwards, the top margin blind can be moved (**3**).

To edit frame properties using a dialog:

1. Select the frame and click **Text Frame Setup** on the Frame context toolbar.

2. From the dialog, you can change the **Number of columns**, **Gutter** distance between columns, **Left Margin**, **Right Margin**, and enable/disable text wrapping around an object.

3. To change the column widths and blinds (top and bottom frame margins), click a cell in the table and enter a new value.

Fitting text to frames

Fitting story text precisely into a sequence of frames is part of the art of laying out publications.

If there's too much story text to fit in a frame sequence, PagePlus stores it in an invisible **overflow area** and the Link button on the last frame of the sequence displays 🔲; an ➕ **AutoFlow** button appears next to the Link button. You might edit the story down or make more room for it by adding an extra frame or two to the sequence. Clicking the AutoFlow button adds additional frames and pages as needed (see below).

Once frames are in position it's still possible to control how text is distributed throughout the frame(s) via tools on the Frame context toolbar.

 The **Text Sizing** flyout offers three tools for controlling how frame text scales through the text frame. These are "one-off" operations (compared to the "continuous" **Autofit** options shown below).

🅰 **Fit Text**
Click to scale the story's text size so it fits exactly into the available frame(s); further text added to the frame will cause text overflow. You can use this early on, to gauge how the story fits, or near the end, to apply the finishing touch. Fit Text first applies small point size changes, then small leading changes, then adjustments to the paragraph space below value, until the text fits.

🔼 **Enlarge Text**
Click to increase the story's text size one increment (approx. 2%).

⌁ **Shrink Text**

Click to reduce the story's text size one increment (approx. 2%).

Each frame's story text can adopt its own individual autofit setting as follows:

 The **AutoFit Options** flyout offers three autofit options which continuously act upon a selected frame's story text.

⌁ **No AutoFit**

This is the normal mode of operation where, if selected, text won't automatically scale throughout the selected text frame, possibly leaving partly empty frames at the end of the frame sequence.

⌁ **Shrink Text on Overflow**

If selected, extra text added to a selected frame will shrink all frame text to avoid text overflow.

A **AutoFit**

If selected, the frame will always scale text automatically by adjusting text size (compare to **Fit Text** which fits text once, with any additional text causing text overflow).

AutoFlow

When importing text, it's a good idea to take advantage of the **AutoFlow** feature, which will automatically create text frames and pages until all the text has been imported. This way, enough frames are created to display the whole story. Then you can gauge just how much adjustment will be needed to fit the story to the available "real estate" in your publication.

If you add more text to a story while editing, or have reduced the size of frame, you may find that an overflow condition crops up. In this case you can decide whether to use AutoFit or click the frame's **AutoFlow** button.

To AutoFlow story text on the page:

- Click  **AutoFlow** just to the left of the frame's  **Link** button.

If no other empty frames are detected, you'll be prompted to autoflow text into a new frame(s) the same size as the original or to new frame(s) sized to the page. If an empty frame exists anywhere in your publication, PagePlus will detect the first empty frame and prompt to flow text into this. At the dialogs, Click Yes to flow into frame or click No to let PagePlus detect and jump to the next empty frame.

Linking text frames

When a text frame is selected, the frame includes a **Link** button at the bottom right which denotes the state of the frame and its story text. It also allows you to control how the frame's story flows to following frames:

No Overflow
The frame is not linked to a following frame (it's either a standalone frame or the last frame in a sequence) and the frame is empty or the end of the story text is visible.

Overflow

The populated frame is not linked (either standalone or last frame) and there is additional story text in the **hidden** overflow area.

An  **Autoflow** button also appears to the left of the **Link** button.

Continued

The frame is linked to a following frame. The end of the story text may be visible, or it may flow into the following frame.

> The button icon will be red if the final frame of the sequence is overflowing, or green if there's no overflow.

There are two basic ways to set up a linked sequence of frames:

- You can link a sequence of empty frames, then import the text.

- You can import the text into a single frame, then create and link additional frames into which the text automatically flows.

> ✎ When frames are created by the **AutoFlow** option (for example when importing text), they are automatically linked in sequence.

To create a link or reorder the links between existing frames, you can use the **Link** button under the frame. Remember to watch the cursor, which changes to indicate these operations.

- You can link to frames already containing text or are already in a link sequence.

- If the frame was not part of a link sequence, its text is merged into the selected text's story.

To link the selected frame to an existing frame:

1. Click the frame's **Link** button (showing ■ or ■.)

2. Click with the Textflow cursor on the frame to be linked to.

To link the selected frame to a newly drawn frame:

- As above, but instead of clicking a "target" frame, either click on the page (for a default frame) or drag across the page (to create a frame sized to your requirements). The latter is ideal for quickly mapping out linked frames across different pages.

To unlink the selected frame from the sequence:

- Click on ■ **Continued**, then click with the Textflow cursor on the same frame.

Story text remains with the "old" frames. For example, if you detach the second frame of a three-frame sequence, the story text remains in the first and third frames, which are now linked into a two-frame story. The detached frame is always empty.

Using artistic text

Artistic text is standalone text you type directly onto a page. Especially useful for headlines, pull quotes, and other special-purpose text, it's easily formatted with the standard text tools.

Here are some differences between frame text and artistic text.

- You can initially "draw" artistic text at a desired point size, and drag it to adjust the size later. Frame text reflows in its frame upon frame resize (but doesn't alter its text size).

- Artistic text can be applied to a **path** but frame text cannot.

- Artistic text won't automatically line wrap like frame text.

- Artistic text doesn't flow or link the way frame text does; the Frame context toolbar's text-fitting functions aren't applicable to artistic text.

To create artistic text:

1. Choose the $\mathbf{A}$ **Artistic Text Tool** from the **Tools** toolbar.

2. Click on the page to make an insertion point from where you'll begin typing.

3. Set initial text properties (style, font, point size, etc.) using the Text context toolbar.

4. Start typing to create the artistic text using your chosen text properties.

To resize or reproportion an artistic text object:

- To resize while maintaining the object's proportions, drag the resize handles.

To resize freely, hold down the **Shift** key while dragging.

To edit artistic text:

- Drag to select a range of text, creating a blue selection.

You can also double-click to select a word, or triple-click to select all text.

Now you can type new text, apply **character and paragraph formatting** (p. 84), edit the text in WritePlus, apply proofing options, and so on.

Putting text on a path

"Ordinary" straight-line **artistic text** is far from ordinary—but you can extend its creative possibilities even further by flowing it along a curved path.

The resulting object has all the properties of artistic text, plus its path is a Bézier curve that you can edit with the Pointer Tool as easily as any other line! In addition, text on a path is editable in some unique ways, as described below.

To apply a preset curved path to text:

1. Create an artistic text object.

2. With the text selected, on the Text context toolbar, click the down arrow on the ✕ ▾ **Preset Text Paths** flyout and choose a preset path.

The text now flows along the specified path, e.g. for "Path - Top Circle".

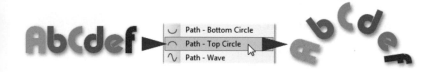

To add artistic text along an existing line or shape:

1. Create a freehand, straight, or curved line (see **Drawing and editing lines** on p. 131) or a shape (see **Drawing and editing shapes** on p. 132).

2. Choose the **A Artistic Text Tool** from the **Tools** toolbar.

3. Bring the cursor very close to the line. When the cursor changes to include a curve, click the mouse where you want the text to begin. Your line appears as a dashed path with an insertion point at its starting end.

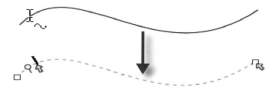

4.   Begin typing at the insertion point. Text flows along the line, which has been converted to a path.

To fit existing text to an existing line or shape:

1.   Create an artistic text object.

2.   Create a freehand, straight, or curved line or a shape.

3.   Select both objects. On the **Tools** menu, choose **Fit Text to Path**. The text now flows along the specified path.

To remove the text path:

1.   Select the path text object.

2.   Click ✕ **Path - None** on the Text context toolbar's Path flyout.

Editing text on the page

You can use the Pointer Tool to edit **frame text**, **table text**, or **artistic text** directly. On the page, you can select and enter text, set paragraph indents and tab stops, change text properties, apply text styles, and use Find and Replace.

Selecting and entering text

The selection of frame text, artistic text, and table text follows the conventions of the most up-to-date word-processing tools. The selection area is shaded in semi-transparent blue for clear editing.

Nulla vestibulum eleifend
nulla. Suspendisse potenti.
Aliquam turpis nisi, venenatis
non, accum san nec, imperdiet
laoreet, lacus.

Double-, triple- or quadruple-click selects a word, paragraph or all text, respectively. You can also make use of the **Ctrl**-click or drag for selection of non-adjacent words, the **Shift** key for ranges of text.

To edit text on the page:

1. Select the Pointer Tool, then click (or drag) in the text object. A standard insertion point appears at the click position.
    - or -
    Select a single word, paragraph or portion of text.

2. Type to insert new text or overwrite selected text, respectively.

    Nulla vestibulum eleifend
    nulla. Suspendisse potenti.
    Aliquam turpis nisi, venenatis
    non, accum san nec, imperdiet
    laoreet, lacus.

To start a new paragraph:

- Press the Return key.

To start a new line within the same paragraph (using a line break or soft return):

- Press **Shift**+Return.

To flow text to the next column (Column Break), frame (Frame Break) or page (Page Break):

- Press **Ctrl**+Return, **Alt**+Return or **Ctrl+Shift**+Return, respectively.

The first two options apply only to frame text. You can use these shortcuts or choose the items from the **Insert>Break** submenu.

To switch between insert mode and overwrite mode:

- Press the **Insert** key.

Checking your text

To ensure your artistic and frame text is error-free and the best copy possible, use the **Spell Checker**, **Proof Reader**, and **Thesaurus** options on the **Tools** menu.

For paragraph indents and tab stops, see PagePlus Help or consider applying indents and tab stops as body text styles (p. 87).

Setting text properties

PagePlus gives you a high degree of typographic control over characters and paragraphs.

To apply basic text formatting:

1. **Select** the text.

2. Use buttons on the Text context toolbar to change text style, font, point size, attributes, paragraph alignment, bullets/numbering, or level.

| Body | Gill Sans MT | 12 pt | **B** *I* <u>U</u> ▾ | *O* ▾ | ≣ ≣ |

To clear local formatting (restore plain/default text properties):

1. Select a range of text with local formatting.

2. Click on the **Clear Formatting** option on the Text context toolbar's text styles drop-down list (or Text Styles tab).

Using fonts

One of the most dramatic ways to change your publication's appearance is to change the fonts used in your artistic text, frame text, or table text.

Font assignment is very simple in PagePlus, and can be done from the Text context toolbar (when text is selected), **Fonts** tab (via **View>Tabs**), or by modifying **text styles** (see p. 89) to use a chosen font.

Using the Fonts tab

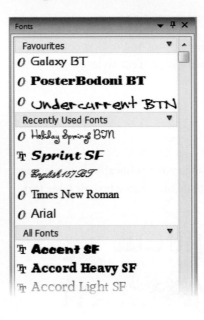

Font assignment is also possible via the **Fonts** tab, which also provides following features:

- Assign fonts to be Websafe or favourites.

- View most recently used, Websafe, and your favourite fonts simultaneously.

- Search for installed fonts via search box.

- Hover-over preview of fonts applied to your document's text (optional).

- Change a font for another throughout your publication or website (by right-click Select All).

The **Fonts** tab is switched off by default. You can switch in on by using **View>Tabs**.

For more information, see PagePlus Help.

Using text styles

PagePlus lets you use named **text styles** (pre-defined or user-defined), which can be applied to **frame text**, **table text**, **artistic text**, index text or table of contents text. A text style is a set of character and/or paragraph attributes saved as a group. When you apply a style to text, you apply the whole group of attributes in just one step. For example, you could use named paragraph styles for particular layout elements, such as "Heading 1" or "Body", and character styles to convey meaning, such as "Emphasis", "Strong", or "Subtle Reference".

Styles can be applied to characters or paragraphs using either the Text context toolbar or the Text Styles tab. Both **paragraph** and **character styles** can be managed from the **Text Style Palette**.

Text style hierarchies

All paragraph or character text styles available in PagePlus are ultimately based on the respective Normal and Default Paragraph Font text styles.

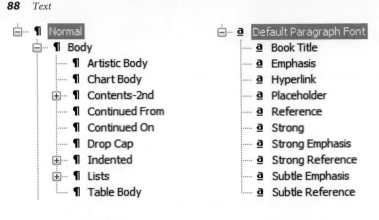

Paragraph styles   *Character styles*

So why have this hierarchy of text styles? The key reason for this is the ability to change a text style at any "level" in the hierarchy in order to affect all "child" styles which belong to it.

Working with named styles

Body ▾ The named style of the currently selected text is displayed in either the **Text Styles** tab or the **Styles** drop-down list on the Text context toolbar. A character style (if one is applied locally) may be shown; otherwise it indicates the paragraph style.

To apply a named style:

1. Using the Pointer Tool, click in a paragraph (if applying a paragraph style) or select a range of text (if applying a character style).

2. Display the **Text Styles** tab and select a style from the style list.
    - or -
    On the Text context toolbar, click the arrow to expand the Styles drop-down list and select a style name.

The Text Style tab highlights the paragraph or character style applied to any selected text.

As both paragraph and character formatting can be applied to the same text, all of the current text's formatting is displayed in the **Current format** box on the tab. In the example below, currently selected text has a 'Strong' character style applied over a 'Body' paragraph style.

Current format: Body + Strong

To update a named style using the properties of existing text:

1. Make your desired formatting changes to any text that uses a named style.

2. On the **Text Styles** tab, right-click the style and choose **Update <style> to Match Selection**.

All text using the named style takes on the new properties.

To modify an existing style:

1. From the Text Styles tab, select 📋 **Manage**, then choose **Modify**.

2. From the Text Style dialog, define (or change) the style name, base style, and any character or paragraph attributes, tabs, bullets, and drop caps.

3. Click **OK** to accept the style, or **Cancel** to abandon changes.

4. Click **Apply** to update text, or click **Close** to maintain the style in the publication for future use.

Alternatively, choose **Text Style Palette** from the **Format** menu to modify styles and to change **text defaults** (see p. 63).

Creating custom text styles

If required, you can create your own custom styles, either based on a currently selected text style or from scratch. See PagePlus Help.

Removing local formatting

To return characters and/or paragraphs back to their original formatting, click on **Clear Formatting** in the **Text Styles** tab. This is great for reverting some formatting which hasn't quite worked out! You can clear the formatting of selected characters, paragraphs, or both depending on what text is currently selected.

$a_{/}$	Clear Character Formatting
$\P_{/}$	Clear Paragraph Formatting
	Clear All Formatting

Like **Clear Formatting**, you can use 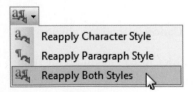 **Reapply Styles** on the **Text Styles** tab (or Text context toolbar) to clear all local overrides leaving the default text. However, where Clear Formatting reverts the text to Normal style, Reapply styles reverts the text back to its current name style.

	Reapply Character Style
	Reapply Paragraph Style
	Reapply Both Styles

Wrapping text

PagePlus lets you wrap frame text around the contours of a separate object, typically around a picture, shape, artistic text, table, or another frame.

Vestibulum semper enim non eros. Sed vitae arcu.
Aliquam erat volutpat. Praesent odio nisl, suscipit
at, rhoncus sit amet,
porttitor sit amet, leo.
Aenean hendrerit est.
Etiam ac augue. Morbi
tincidunt neque ut lacus.
Duis vulputate cursus
orci. Mauris justo lorem,
scelerisque sit amet, placerat sed,
condimentum in, leo. Donec urna est, semper
quis, auctor eget, ultrices in, purus. Etiam rutrum.

To wrap text around an object:

1. Select the object around which you want the text to wrap.

2. Click the ▣ **Wrap Settings** button on the **Arrange** toolbar.

3. Select how text will wrap by clicking a sample.

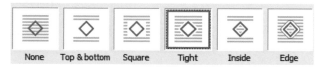

| None | Top & bottom | Square | Tight | Inside | Edge |

4. Choose which side(s) the wrapping method will be applied.

Wrap To

| All | Both sides | Left | Right | Largest side |

5. Click **OK**.

In addition, you can specify the **Distance from text**: the "standoff" between the object's **wrap outline** and adjacent text. (The wrap outline is a contour that defines the object's edges for text wrapping purposes.) Different object types have different initial wrap outlines.

You can manually adjust the wrap outline using the Curve context toolbar for more precise text fitting. See PagePlus help for more information.

Creating a bulleted or numbered list

You can turn a series of paragraphs into **bulleted**, **numbered** or **multi-level lists**. Bullets are especially useful when listing items of interest in no specific order of preference, numbered lists for presenting step-by-step procedures (by number or letter), and multi-level lists for more intelligent hierarchical lists with prefixed numbers, symbols, or a mix of both, all with supporting optional text (see **Using multi-level lists** on p. 94).

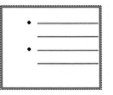

| *Bulleted list* | *Numbered list* | *Multi-level list* |

Lists can be applied to normal text (as local formatting) or to **text styles** equally.

To create a simple bulleted or numbered list:

1. Select one or more paragraphs.

    - or -

    Click in a paragraph's text.

2.   Select ☰ **Bulleted List** or ☰ **Numbered List** from the Text context toolbar.

To create a bulleted or numbered list (using presets):

1.   Select one or more paragraphs.
     - or -
     Click in a paragraph's text.

2.   Select **Bullets and Numbering** from the **Format** menu.

3.   From the Text Style dialog's Bullets and Numbering menu option, choose **Bullet**, **Number**, or **Multi-Level** from the **Style** drop-down list.

4.   Select one of the preset formats shown by default.
     - or -
     For a custom list, click the **Details** button to display, then alter custom options.

5.   Click **OK** to apply list formatting.

> For number and multi-level lists, check **Restart numbering** to restart numbering from the current cursor position in the list; otherwise, leave the option unchecked.

Using multi-level lists

For multi-level lists you can set a different character (symbol, text or number) to display at each level of your list. Levels are normally considered to be subordinate to each other, where Level 1 (first level), Level 2 (second), Level 3 (third), etc. are of decreasing importance in the list. For example, the simple multi-level numbered passage of text opposite is arranged at three levels.

If you apply a multi-level preset to a range of text you'll get a list with the preset's Level 1 format applied by default. Unless you use **text styles**, you'll have to change to levels 2, 3, 4, etc. to set the correct level for your list entry.

Changing list levels on selected paragraphs:

- Click the ⊞ **Increase Paragraph Indent** or ⊞ **Decrease Paragraph Indent** button on the Text context toolbar to increment or decrement the current level by one.

The multi-level presets offer some simple but commonly used schemes for paragraph list formatting. However, if you want to create your own lists or modify an existing list (your own or a preset), use the **Details** button in the Text Style dialog when Multi-Level style is selected. See PagePlus Help for more details.

Assigning bullets, numbers, and levels to styles

PagePlus lets you easily associate any bulleted, numbered or multi-level list style (either preset or custom list) to an existing text style (see p. 87).

Inserting user details

When you **create a publication from a design template** for the first time, you may be prompted to update your user details (Name, Company, Telephone number, etc.) in a User Details dialog. These details will automatically populate pre-defined text "fields" in your publication, making it personalized.

PagePlus supports **business sets** (i.e., stored sets of user details) which can be created per customer and applied to your publication. This lets you create publication variants, with each differing just in their user details. You can choose which set to use when you start with a new design template (or at any time during your session).

To add, edit or change user details:

1.   Click the 👥 **User Details** button on the Pages context toolbar (deselect objects to view).

2.   Enter new information into the spaces on the **Business Sets** or **Home** tab (a **Calendars** tab will appear if there is a calendar in your publication).

3.   Click **Update**.

Inserting your own fields

If you're **starting from scratch** (p. 19), you can also insert one or more User Details fields into your publication.

To insert a User Detail field:

1.   Select the Pointer Tool and click in the text for an insertion point.

2.   From the **Insert** menu, select **Information>User Details**.

3.   Select a user detail entry and optionally any text **Prefix** or **Suffix** to include with your user details, e.g. *(Home) Name*.

4.   Click **OK**.

For existing publications, the fields (once edited) can be updated or swapped as described previously.

Tables, Charts, and Calendars

7

Creating tables

Tables are ideal for presenting text and data in a variety of easily customizable row-and-column formats, with built-in spreadsheet capabilities.

Region	J	F	M	A	M	J	J	A	S	O	N	D	Sum
N	12	8	7	9	11	8	18	11	3	11	22	16	136
S	6	6	7	10	14	12	11	13	7	13	14	10	123
W	12	6	5	20	9	18	17	14	10	14	13	18	156

Rather than starting from scratch, PagePlus is supplied with a selection of pre-defined table formats, called **AutoFormats**, that can be used. Simply pick one and fill in the cells with content.

PagePlus lets you:

- Edit the pre-defined format before adding a new table to the page.

- Create your own custom formats without creating a table. See Creating custom table formats in PagePlus Help.

- Edit existing tables to fit a different format (pre-defined or custom).

To create a table:

1. On the **Tools** toolbar, choose the **Table Tool** from the **Table** flyout.

2. Click on the page or pasteboard, or drag to set the table's dimensions. The **Create Table** dialog opens with a selection of preset table formats shown in the **Format** window.

3. Step through the list to preview the layouts and select one. To begin with a plain table, select **(Default)**.

4. (Optional) Click **Edit** if you want to further customize your chosen format.

5. Set the **Table Size**. This is the number of rows and columns that make up the table layout.

6. Click **OK**. The new table appears on the page.

Flowing tables

It is possible to create tables that can be split into multiple parts on the same page or even across multiple pages. This is useful if you're planning to present a large amount of table data or if you're constrained by your existing page design; for either reason, table placement becomes that much easier.

Region	J	F	M	A	M	J
N	12	8	7	9	11	8
S	6	6	7	10	14	12
W	12	6	5	20	9	18

J	A	S	O	N	D	Sum
18	11	3	11	22	16	136
11	13	7	13	14	10	123
17	14	10	14	13	18	156

Even though physically split, each table portion still maintains a link with previous and next tables. This allows additional rows or columns to be added, with the table reflowing subsequent rows or columns.

You can design your flowing table from scratch or split up an existing table already on the page.

To create a flowing table from scratch:

1. Create your table as described in **Creating tables** (p. 99).

2. [icons] On the control bar under your selected table, click **Flow Down** to create a linked table based on extra rows, or **Flow Right** for a linked table based on extra columns.

If you've a table that you've created previously or you're redesigning your table layout, you can split it by row or column.

To split up an existing flowing table:

1. Select the table.

2. Hover over the arrows shown at the bottom-centre or right-centre of these.

3. Drag these arrows up or left, respectively, to split by row or column.

The rows or columns hidden by dragging will pop up as a linked table on mouse release.

To navigate between linked tables:

- [icons] On the control bar, under your selected table, click **Next Table** or **Previous Table**.

To rejoin tables:

1. Select a linked table to which you want to rejoin the next table in the linked sequence.

2. On the control bar, click 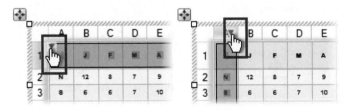 **Rejoin**.

For flowing tables it's a great idea to repeat the initial table's row or column headers on each linked table. This is essential for correct referencing of table data.

Row or column headers are repeated on all linked tables based on extra rows (Flow down) or columns (Flow right). You can't repeat row and column headers in the same linked table sequence.

To repeat row/column headers:

1. Select the initial table in the table flow.

2. Click the drop-down arrow, displayed on hover over in the row/column header (shown as '1' and 'A' below).

3. Select **Repeat as Header** from the submenu.

The row or column header is repeated on the linked table.

Using charts

For any small business, club, or school project, the ability to present important data professionally will impress your audience, and potentially gain support for your activities.

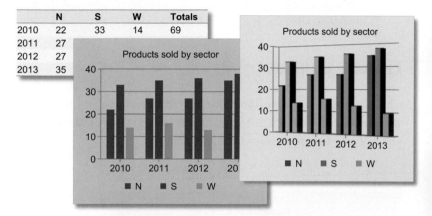

	N	S	W	Totals
2010	22	33	14	69
2011	27			
2012	27			
2013	35			

Tables and charts are intrinsically linked in PagePlus. If you need a recap on tables, see **Creating tables** on p. 99. PagePlus also lets you create multiple charts from the same table data using the **Chart Data** tab.

Chart types

PagePlus provides a range of popular chart types, each designed to present data differently. All you need to do is select a chart that suits the type of data you wish to present.

Area chart

Bar chart

Column chart

Line chart

Pie chart

Scatter chart (XY)

The above chart types are also available in 3D (as extrusions of the 2D chart types).

Charts explained

Charts are made up of specific elements. Once you learn how to manipulate each element using the **Charts** tab and **Chart Data** tab, you'll be able to create powerful charts easily.

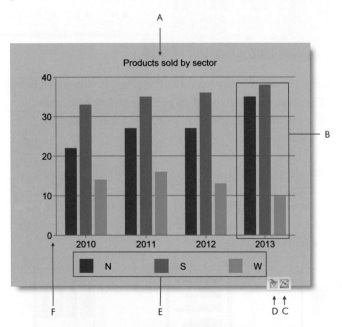

(A) Chart Title, (B) Series, (C) Go to Chart Data link, (D) Go to Associated Table link, (E) Series Legend, (F) Chart Area.

Data sources

The first step in creating charts is to consider what data you'll want to base your chart on. You should spend some time in advance preparing data for chart presentation.

Several data sources can be used to base your chart on. Here's an overview of typical data sources that will let you create charts easily.

Data source	Description
Chart Data tab	Using PagePlus's Chart Data tab, you can either:
	• Create your own off-the-page chart data without the need for a PagePlus table. See **Creating charts from scratch** on p. 106.
	-or -
	• Create chart variations (of differing type and data ranges) from a single PagePlus table.
PagePlus table	If you have a PagePlus publication which already has a table present, you can base your chart on that table data, with the option of presenting table and chart data in unison. See **Creating charts from PagePlus tables** on p. 107.
External spreadsheet	You can paste cell data from Microsoft Excel directly onto your **page or pasteboard**. Once in PagePlus, you can create a chart as you would with a PagePlus table (see above).

If you want to use table data from Microsoft Word, copy and paste the table into Excel first.

Creating charts from scratch

PagePlus provides the **Chart Tool** to place a chart onto your page. Initially a placeholder chart, it can be populated with real chart data from the **Chart Data** tab. The tab lets you store and develop your chart data "off-page" without cluttering up your page design.

The chart can be designed and later modified by using a Chart context toolbar displayed above your workspace when the chart is selected.

To create a chart from scratch:

1.    From the **Tools** toolbar's **Table Tools** flyout, select **Chart Tool**.

2.   On the context toolbar, from the **Chart** drop-down list, select a chart type.

3.   Click on the page or drag out the chart to the desired size.

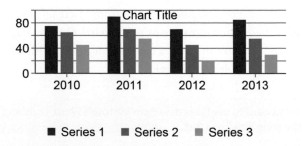

At this point, the chart is just a placeholder, using sample data automatically added to the **Chart Data** tab. You can edit this sample data using your own data, name your row/column headers, and even add extra rows and columns to suit additional chart data—by default, each row represents a separate colour-coded series component.

To edit data in the Chart Data tab:

1.   Click [icon] **Chart Data** under the selected chart.

     The Chart Data tab displays temporarily in the workspace.

2.   On the **Chart Data** tab, click in each cell and enter data as appropriate.

     The chart will update with the newly entered values.

3.   Replace the row and numeric column headers (i.e., Series 1, 2, and 3; and 1, 2, 3, 4, respectively) with real names. These will update in your chart immediately.

	1	2	3	4
■ Series 1	75	90	70	85
■ Series 2				
■ Series 3				

	2010	2011	2012	2013
■ N	75	90	70	85
■ S	65	70	45	55
■ W	45	55	20	30

Creating charts (from PagePlus tables)

If you already have a table in your publication you can create a chart based on the entire table, rows, columns, or selected ranges.

To create a chart from a PagePlus table:

1.   Select the table (click the bounding box around the table).

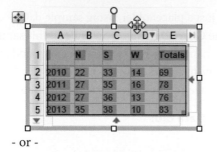

- or -

Select a row or column by clicking in a row or column header.

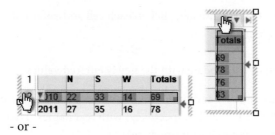

- or -

For selected ranges, drag across rows and columns to set your range.

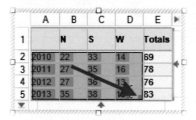

2.   On the control bar under the table, click ▮▮ **Chart Tool**.

3.   Position the ⁻ᵢ⁻ cursor, and drag across the page to create your chart.

On the Chart context toolbar above your workspace, you can modify the chart with respect to chart type, stacking options, data range, and series presentation.

To navigate from selected table to chart:

- Under the table, click 🔳 **Go to Associated Chart**.
  - or -

- 🔳 If you have multiple charts based on the same table, click **Go to Associated Chart** and then select a chart from flyout.

To navigate from selected chart to table:

- Under the chart, click 🔳 **Go to Associated Table**.

Modifying charts

It is possible that you may want to change how your chart is presented. The Chart context toolbar gives you the freedom to swap between chart types, base your chart on different ranges, and toggle series as row or columns.

Editing titles

To edit your chart title:

- Click on the chart title and begin typing.

Formatting and styling charts

The **Charts** tab serves a dual purpose in PagePlus—to fine tune the chart's look and to manage how the series are used in your chart.

In addition, the **Styles** tab can be used to apply a completely new look to your chart, even swapping the chart type.

To display the Charts tab:

- At the bottom of your right-hand tab group, click **Charts**.

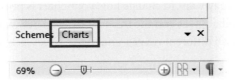

The tab offers three buttons called Chart, Axes, and Series.

- **Chart**: Used for title and series legend control and positioning. Other options are the same as provided on the Chart context toolbar.

- **Axes**: The Axes section adds axis-specific titles, labels, guides, and any other chart elements that aid the interpretation of chart data.

- **Series**: Modifies individual series, including manually assigning series labels, series plotting, enabling trendlines, error bars, and value labels.

For an easy way to transform your chart's appearance in one click, you can use the **Styles tab**. Each preset thumbnail stores separate style settings such as type, and style attributes of titles, series legends, axes, and series.

To apply a style to your chart:

1. On the **Styles** tab, select the **Charts** category from the drop-down list.

2. Click on a style preset thumbnail.

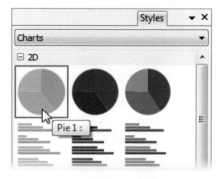

To change colours in your chart:

- Select the chart's background or any series component, then select a colour from the **Colour** tab or **Swatches** tab.

Inserting a calendar

The **Calendar Wizard** helps you design month-at-a-glance calendars for use in your publication.

The calendar is created as a scalable **text-based table** so you can edit text using the standard text tools. The properties of a selected calendar are similar to those of a table, and can be modified identically.

You can complement public holiday listings (e.g., Bank holidays) by adding personal events such as birthdays, anniversaries, and bill payments (unfortunately!) so that the events show up on your calendar.

To insert a calendar:

1.   Click the Table flyout on the **Tools** toolbar and choose **Insert Calendar**.

2.   Drag acrosss the page to set the desired size of the calendar.

3.   From the displayed **Calendar Wizard**, define options for your calendar including setting the year and month, calendar style (square, or in single or double column format), week start day, room to write, display options, switching on personal events/holidays, and calendar format.

4.   Click **Finish** to complete the wizard.

To view and edit a selected calendar's properties:

- Click   **Edit Calendar** on the Calendar context toolbar.

To add an event to a selected calendar:

- Click   **Calendar Events** on the context toolbar.

August 2013		
1	T	
2	F	
3	S	
4	S	Laura's birthday
5	M	Summer Bank Holiday(Scot.)
6	T	
7	W	
8	T	Holiday Leave
9	F	
10	S	Presentation (am)
11	S	Bank Manager 10.00am
12	M	

Pictures

8

Adding picture frames

Picture frames let you present your pictures in a decorative surround, much like you'd show off your favourite picture in a picture frame in your home. You can select from an impressive collection of professionally designed picture frames, and simply drag them onto your publication page before filling them with pictures.

Picture frames are **assets**, along with graphics, pictures, page elements, backgrounds, and are **browsed for** (and managed) in the same way as any other asset. See **Using assets** on p. 43.

To add a picture frame:

1. From the Assets tab, select **Browse**.

2. In the **Asset Browser** dialog, select **Picture Frames** from the **Categories** section.

▲ **Categories**
- 🖫 Graphics
- 🖼 Pictures
- ☐ Picture Frames
- 🖻 Page Content
- ⬛ Backgrounds
- 🗐 Pages

3. Navigate the themed sub-categories to locate a picture frame, then select an individual frame or click **Add All** ☑ to include all the frames from the sub-category. A check mark will appear on selected thumbnails.

4. Click **Close**. The frame(s) appears in the **Assets** tab (Picture Frames category).

5. Drag a chosen frame thumbnail to your page.

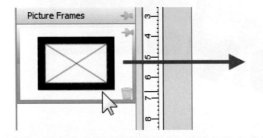

🖳 Empty picture frames are shown as envelope-shaped placeholders on the page.

To add a borderless picture frame:

1. ⊠ 🖼 ▾ Select **Rectangular Picture Frame** on the **Tools** toolbar's **Picture** flyout.

    - or -

    Select **Picture>Empty Frame** from the **Insert** menu.

2. The mouse pointer changes to the **Picture Paste** cursor. What you do next determines the initial size and placement of the picture frame.

- To insert the frame at a default size, simply click the mouse.
  - or -

- To set the size of the frame, drag out a region and release the mouse button. If needed, use the **Shift** key while dragging to maintain aspect ratio (to a square).

To add a picture to a frame (and vice versa):

- From the Assets tab (Pictures category), drag and drop a picture directly onto the picture frame.
  - or -

- From the Assets tab (Picture Frames category), drag and drop a picture frame directly onto an already placed picture.

The picture is added to the frame using default Picture Frame properties, i.e. it is scaled to maximum fit; aspect ratio is always maintained. However, you can alter the picture's size, orientation, positioning, and scaling relative to its frame.

To change picture size and positioning:

 All selected picture frames that contain a picture will display a supporting **Picture frame** toolbar under the frame. This offers panning, rotation (90 degrees anti-clockwise), zoom in, zoom out, and replace picture controls).

To change picture scaling and alignment:

1. Select the picture frame and choose ▦ **Frame Properties** on the Picture context toolbar.

2. In the dialog, you can scale to maximum/minimum, Stretch to Fit, or use the original image's size (No Scale).

3. To change vertical alignment of pictures within the frames, select **Top**, **Middle**, or **Bottom**.

4. For horizontal alignment, select **Left**, Centre, or **Right**.

Creating shaped picture frames

While you can take advantage of PagePlus's preset frames you can create your own shape (e.g., a morphed QuickShape or closed curve) then convert it to a picture frame.

To create a shaped picture frame:

1. Create a **closed shape** or **QuickShapes** (p. 135 and p. 133, respectively).

2. Right-click the shape and select **Convert To>Picture Frame**.

You can then add a picture to the frame as described previously.

> ✎ Any object you've designed that contains a "hole" can be converted to a picture frame using the above method.
>
> ✎ To store the picture frame for reuse globally or just in the publication, drag to the Assets tab's My Designs or Picture Frames category. For the latter, if you close the publication, you'll be asked if you want to save the frame to an asset pack.

Adding pictures

The **Assets** tab (Pictures category) acts as a "basket" for initially gathering together and then including pictures in your publication. Its chief use is to aid the design process by improving efficiency (avoiding having to import pictures one by one) and convenience (making pictures always-at-hand). For picture-rich documents in particular, the tab is a valuable tool for dragging pictures directly into **bordered** or **unbordered** picture frames or for simply replacing existing pictures on the page.

PagePlus also lets you insert pictures from a wide variety of file formats, such as bitmaps, vector images, and metafiles (including Serif Metafiles).

For photos from your digital camera, you can simply navigate to the folder containing your already downloaded photos (i.e., on your hard disk) and include them in the tab. Similarly, scanned images already saved to your hard disk can be added by this method.

Adding pictures to the Assets tab

To add pictures to the tab:

1. Select the Assets tab's Pictures category, and click **Add.**

2. From the dialog, navigate to a folder, and select your picture(s).

3. Click **Open**. Your pictures appear as thumbnails within the Assets tab's Picture category.

Adding pictures to the page

Pictures can be added to your publication by dragging directly onto your page.

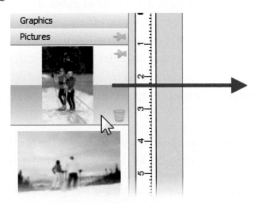

To add a picture to your page:

- From the Assets tab (Pictures category), drag a picture thumbnail directly onto the page, inline into artistic/frame text (at a chosen insertion point), or into a picture frame. Once added, the picture thumbnail indicates the number of times the picture has been used in the publication (①).

> When placed, pictures are linked to your project by default and not embedded. Photos can be embedded instead on import via the **Tools** toolbar or at any time using the Resource Manager.

If you've positioned empty picture frames you can use **AutoFlow** to automatically populate them with pictures.

AutoFlow—adding content automatically

AutoFlow lets you flow the pictures present in the tab's Pictures category throughout empty picture **frames** spread throughout your publication (you can't reflow pictures once frames are populated with content).

Rearrange picture order prior to autoflow by using drag and drop.

To automatically flow your pictures:

- Click **AutoFlow** at the bottom of the Assets tab (Pictures category). The pictures are placed sequentially in your document's available picture frames in the order they appear in the tab (reorder beforehand if needed).

Adding pictures with resizing and embed/link control

As well as dragging a picture thumbnail from the Assets tab, pictures can be added to PagePlus by copy and paste or dragging a file from an external Windows folder directly onto your page.

PagePlus also lets you import pictures via **Import Picture** on the **Tools** toolbar. You'll be able to size the picture and embed/link the picture in your publication. See PagePlus Help for more information.

Cropping pictures

PagePlus includes the **Square Crop Tool** and **Irregular Crop Tool** which are used typically for cropping pictures on the page. Cropping discards unwanted "outer" regions of a picture while keeping the remainder visible.

To crop a picture (square crop):

1. Select a picture and then on the **Attributes** toolbar, click the **Square Crop Tool**.

2. Hover over an edge or corner.

3. Drag the cursor inwards (down, left or right) on your picture.

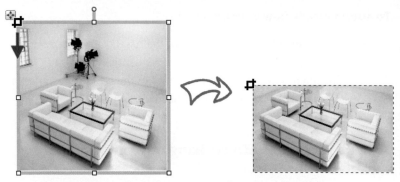

4. Repeat with other edge or corner handles, if needed.

5. (Optional) From the context toolbar, set a **Feather** value for a soft edge.

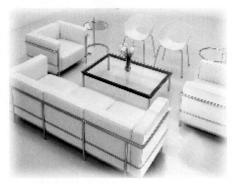

To crop a picture (irregular crop)

1. With the **Square Crop Tool** selected, select the **Irregular Crop Tool** above your workpace.

2. The Curve context toolbar appears on its right, which lets you control the displayed nodes and connecting segments that define the object's crop outline.

6. To move a node (control point) where you see the $^{-}\overline{\mathstrut}_{\mathstrut}^{-}$ cursor, drag the node.

   - or -

   To move a line segment (between two nodes) where you see the cursor, drag the segment.

   - or -

   Add extra nodes by double-clicking on the crop outline, then reposition them.

> To scale the object within the crop outline, press the **Ctrl** key, click your left mouse button, then move your mouse upwards or downwards.

> If you add **picture frames** to your publication, you can position your placed picture using pan and zoom instead of using the Square Crop Tool.

Cropping pictures to shapes

The **Crop to Shape** command lets you create shaped pictures from drawn closed shapes (below) or silhouettes placed over your picture. The picture gets clipped to the outline of the shape, leaving a shape equivalent to the overlapping region.

To crop a picture using shapes:

1. Place the shape in front of the picture to be cropped, using the **Arrange** menu and/or **Arrange** toolbar as needed.

2. With both objects selected (or grouped), choose **Crop to Shape** from the **Tools** menu.

You can restore an object cropped in this way to its original shape, but the upper "cropping" object is permanently deleted (use **Undo** to recover it if necessary).

Using Cutout Studio

Cutout Studio offers a powerful integrated solution for cutting objects out from their backgrounds. Depending on the make up of your images you can separate subject of interests from their backgrounds, either by retaining the subject of interest (usually people, objects, etc.) or removing a simple uniform background (e.g., sky, studio backdrop). In both instances, the resulting "cutout" image creates an eye-catching look for your publication.

The latter background removal method is illustrated in the following multi-image example.

The initial green background is discarded, leaving interim checkerboard transparency, from which another image can be used as a more attractive background. A red tint on the second image's background is used to indicate areas to be discarded.

To launch Cutout Studio:

1. Select a picture to be cut out.

2. Select **Cutout Studio** from the displayed Picture context toolbar. Cutout Studio is launched.

Choose an output

By default an alpha-edged bitmap is created by cutting out, but's possible to change the **Output Type** prior to selecting areas for keeping/discarding.

Output Type

| Alpha-edged Bitmap ▼ |
| Alpha-edged Bitmap |
| Vector-cropped Bitmap |

Blur   25

The choice you make really depends on the picture. A vector-edged bitmap is better for cutting out pictures with well defined edges.

> 💡 Zoom into your image to examine its edges; this may influence the output type chosen.

Selecting areas to keep or discard

A pair of brushes for keeping and discarding is used to "paint" areas of the image. The tools are called **Keep Brush** and **Discard Brush**, and are either used independently or, more typically, in combination with each other. When using either tool, the brush paints an area contained by an outline which is considered to be retained or discarded (depending on brush type). A configurable number of pixels adjacent to the outline area are blended.

To select image areas for keeping/discarding:

1. In Cutout Studio, click either **Keep Brush Tool** or **Discard Brush Tool** from the left of the Studio workspace.

2. (Optional) Pick a **Brush size** for the area to be worked on.

3. (Optional) Set a **Grow Tolerance** value to automatically expand the selected area under the cursor (by detecting colours similar to those within the current selection). The greater the value the more the selected area will grow. Uncheck the option to switch the feature off.

4. Using the circular cursor, click and drag across the area to be retained or discarded (depending on Keep or Discard Brush Tool selection). It's OK to repeatedly click and drag until your selection area is made.

The **Undo** button reverts to the last made selection.

To fine-tune your selection, you can switch between Keep and Discard brushes by temporarily holding down the **Alt** key.

5.   If you're outputting an alpha-edged bitmap, you can refine the area to be kept/discarded within Cutout Studio (only after previewing) with Erase and Restore **touch-up tools**. Vector-cropped images can be cropped using standard PagePlus crop tools outside of the Studio.

6.   Click   **OK** to create your cutout.

You'll see your image in your publication in its original location, but with the selected areas cut away (made transparent).

Adjustments and effects

For any selected picture, the Picture context toolbar is displayed to offer various commonly used photo editing tools.

The PhotoLab and *Cutout Studio* options offer Studio-based multiple adjustment/effect management and background/foreground removal, respectively. The Edit in PhotoPlus option lets you edit your picture in Serif's PhotoPlus photo-editing program.

Simple adjustments

The above toolbar also lets you remove the red-eye effect and fine-tune brightness, contrast, and levels.

To remove red eye:

- **Zoom into** the subject's eyes, click   **Remove Red Eye**, then click the cursor over the red eye.

To decrease/increase brightness:

- Click **Decrease Brightness** or **Increase Brightness**.

To decrease/increase contrast:

- Click **Decrease Contrast** or **Increase Contrast**.

To automatically adjust the tonal range (levels) and contrast:

- Click **Auto Level Tonal Range** or **Auto Contrast**.

For a studio-based approach to making picture adjustments and effects, see Applying PhotoLab filters in PagePlus Help.

Lines and Shapes

9

Drawing and editing lines

The **Tools** toolbar provides **Pencil**, **Straight Line**, and **Pen** tools for drawing freehand, straight, and curved/straight lines, respectively.

The  **Pencil Tool** lets you sketch curved lines and shapes in a **freeform** way. See PagePlus Help for more details.

The  **Pen Tool** lets you join a series of line segments (which may be **curved** or **straight**) using "connect the dots" mouse clicks. See PagePlus Help for more details.

The **Straight Line Tool** is for drawing **straight** lines (for example, drawn in the column gutter to separate columns); rules at the top and/or bottom of the page; or horizontal lines to separate sections or highlight headlines.

> Any curved line can be closed (by joining line ends) to create a custom **shape** (see **Drawing and editing shapes** on p. 132 for details).

Editing lines

Use the Pointer Tool in conjunction with the context toolbar to adjust lines once you've drawn them. The techniques are the same whether you're editing a separate line object or the outline of a closed shape.

When selected, each line type shows square nodes which can be used for **reshaping** lines.See PagePlus Help for information on editing lines.

Drawing and editing shapes

QuickShapes are pre-designed objects of widely varying shapes that you can instantly add to your page.

Once you've drawn a QuickShape, you can morph its original shape using control handles, and adjust its properties—for example, by applying **gradient or bitmap fills** (including your own bitmap pictures!) or **transparency effects**.

Another way to create a shape is to **draw a line** and then connect its start and end nodes, creating a **closed shape**.

QuickShapes

The QuickShape flyout contains a wide variety of commonly used shapes, including boxes, ovals, arrows, polygons, stars, cubes, and cylinders.

You can easily turn shapes into web **buttons** by adding hyperlinks or overlaying hotspots. The "Quick Button" (indicated) is especially intended for creating stylish button outlines!

It's also possible to use the context toolbar situated above the workspace to adjust a QuickShape's line weight, colour, style, and more. New shapes always take the default line and fill (initially a black line with a white fill).

To create a QuickShape:

1. Click the ▢ ▾ **QuickShape** flyout on the **Tools** toolbar and select a shape from the flyout.

2. Click on the page to create a new shape at a default size.
    - or -
    Drag across the page to size your shape. When the shape is the right size, release the mouse button.

To draw a constrained shape (such as a circle):

- Hold down the **Shift** key as you drag.

All QuickShapes can be **positioned**, **resized**, **rotated**, and **filled**. What's more, you can morph them using adjustable sliding handles around the QuickShape. Each shape changes in a logical way to allow its exact appearance to be altered. The ability to alter the appearance of

QuickShape objects makes them more flexible and convenient than clipart pictures with similar designs. For example:

- Dragging the handles on a Polygon will change the number of sides to make a triangle, pentagon, hexagon, or other polygon.

- Dragging the handles on a Rectangle alters the box corners to make them more or less rounded.

- Dragging the handles of an Ellipse will convert it into a "pie" shape.

To adjust the appearance of a QuickShape:

1. Click on the QuickShape to reveal one or more sliding handles around the shape. These are distinct from the "inner" selection handles. Different QuickShapes have different handles which have separate functions.

2. To change the appearance of a QuickShape, drag its handles.

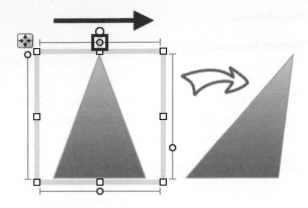

Closed shapes

As soon as you draw or select a line, you'll see the line's nodes appear. Nodes show the end points of each segment in the line. Freehand curves typically have many nodes; straight or curved line segments have only two. You can make a shape by extending a line back to its starting point.

To turn a selected line into a shape:

* Select the line with the **Pointer Tool** and then click ⊹ **Close Curve** on the context toolbar.

You can go the other way, too—break open a shape in order to add one or more line segments.

To break open a line or shape:

1. With the **Pointer Tool**, select the node where you want to break the shape.

2. Click the ⇟ **Break Curve** button on the context toolbar. The shape will become a line, with the selected node split into two nodes, one at each end of the new line.

3. You can now use the **Pointer Tool** to reshape the line as needed.

See PagePlus Help for more information on editing shapes.

Saving custom shapes

Having taken time to create your custom shapes, you may wish to reuse them in future projects. The **Assets** tab provides the ideal location for storing your custom shapes for later use. Simply drag from the page into the tab's Graphics category.

Effects and Styles

10

Applying effects

PagePlus provides a variety of **effects** that you can use to enhance any object. **2D** effects such as drop shadows, feather, bevels, emboss are popular, along with **3D** effects for more sophisticated textured surface effects.

Both 2D and 3D effects can be applied individually (or in combination) using the **Effects** tab.

2D effects

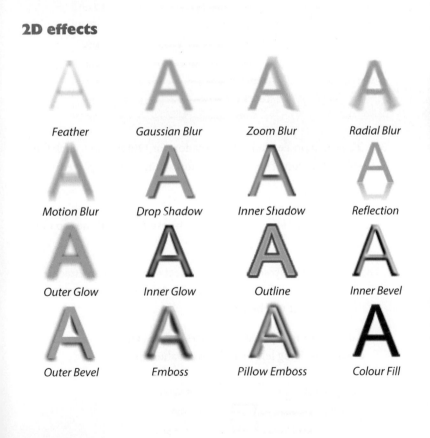

Feather	Gaussian Blur	Zoom Blur	Radial Blur
Motion Blur	Drop Shadow	Inner Shadow	Reflection
Outer Glow	Inner Glow	Outline	Inner Bevel
Outer Bevel	Emboss	Pillow Emboss	Colour Fill

To apply 2D effects:

1. Select an object.

2. Display the Effects tab by clicking its tab name (presented vertically at the right of your screen by default).

3. To switch on Feather, Drop Shadow, or Outer Glow, click the effect's ☐ icon. The effect's default settings are displayed.

    - or -

    i. For other effects, click ⚙ **Choose Effects** at the top of the tab.

    ii. From the flyout, select **2D Effects** and select an effect from the submenu. The effect is added to the tab, and its entry in the flyout will be checked.

4. Adjust settings by altering sliders, values, check boxes, or drop-down lists. Drag left or right over values to adjust.

As you change settings, the effect on the page updates automatically.

To switch off an effect:

- Click the effect's ◼ icon on its title bar. Note that your adjusted settings are kept but are switched off.

To reset an effect back to default:

- Click the effect's ↖ icon on its title bar.

To remove an effect from the tab:

- Click ✦ **Choose Effects** at the top of the tab, then click to uncheck the effect's entry on the flyout. If the effect is applied to a selected object(s) it will be removed from the object.

Using favourites

To apply effects using favourites:

1. On the Effects tab, click ☆ **Favourites** on the chosen effect's title bar.

2. On the displayed gallery, select an effect thumbnail.

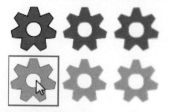

To view the default settings view, click ⚙ **Settings**.

To save a custom effect to your favourites:

1.   Adjust settings for your chosen effect.

2.   On the effect's title bar, click ☆ **Add Favourite**. Your effect is saved to the favourites gallery.

3D Effects

3D effects go beyond 2D effects (such as shadow, glow, bevel, and emboss effects) to create the impression of a textured surface on the object itself. You can use the **Effects** tab to apply one or more 3D effects to the same object.

You'll find that some effects are used in combination to create realistic surface effects such as glass.

To apply 3D effects:

1.   Select an object.

2.   Display the Effects tab by clicking its tab name (presented vertically at the right of your screen by default).

3.   Click 🔲 **Choose Effects** at the top of the tab.

4. From the flyout, select **3D Effects** and select an effect from the submenu. The effect is added to the tab.

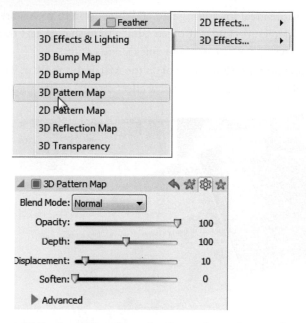

5. Add further effects from the flyout depending on the type of effect you want.

6. Adjust settings for 3D effects by altering sliders, values, check boxes, or drop-down lists.

The **3D Effects & Lighting** category hosts master control settings which are enabled when any 3D effect is applied.

Using the Shadow Tool

Shadows are great for adding flair and dimension to your work, particularly to pictures and text objects, but also to shapes, text frames and tables. To help you create them quickly and easily, PagePlus provides the **Shadow Tool** on the **Attributes** toolbar. The tool affords freeform control of the shadow effect directly on the page.

For more creative shadows, the tool lets you apply skewed shadows, again directly on the page.

Adjustment of shadow colour, opacity, blur, and scaling/distance is possible using controllable nodes directly on the page (or via a supporting Shadow context toolbar).

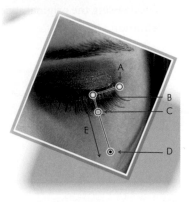

(**A**) *Blur,* (**B**) *Shadow origin,* (**C**) *Opacity,* (**D**) *Colour,* (**E**) *Scaling*

Once you've created a shadow, you can also fine-tune it as needed using the **Effects** tab.

Using object styles

The **Styles** tab contains multiple galleries of pre-designed styles that you can apply to any object, or customize to suit your own taste! Galleries exist in effect categories including Blurs, 3D, Edge, Warps, Materials and more, with each category having further subcategories.

3D surface and texture presets are available in various categories (Presets - Default, Presets - Fun, Presets - Materials, and Texture).

> Styles store fill, transparency, line/text properties, and effects under a single style name, making it easy to apply combinations of attributes to an object in one click.

At a later date, if you edit the style, all objects using the original style will update automatically to the new style definition.

To apply an object style to a selected object(s):

1. Display the **Styles** tab.

2. Expand the drop-down menu to select a named style category (e.g., Presets - Default), then pick a subcategory (e.g., Mixed) by scrolling the lower window.

3. Preview available styles as thumbnails in the window.

4. Click a style thumbnail to apply that style.

To unlink an object from its style definition:

- Right-click the object and choose **Format>Object Style>Unlink**.

To create a custom object style:

- Right-click the object and choose **Format>Object Style>Create**.

See Creating custom object styles in PagePlus Help for more information.

Colour, Fills, and Transparency

11

Applying solid fills

PagePlus offers a number of ways to apply solid colour fills to objects of different kinds:

- You can apply solid colours to an object's **line** or **fill**. As you might expect, QuickShapes and closed shapes (see **Drawing and editing shapes** on p. 132) have both line and fill properties, whereas straight and freehand lines have only a line property.

- Characters in text objects can have a background fill, line, and text colour (i.e., for highlighting, text outlines, and the text fill itself). Text frames and table cells can have a background fill independent of the characters they contain.

To apply a solid colour via the Colour tab or Swatches tab:

1. Select the object(s) or highlight a range of text.

2. ▟ ▢ **A** Select the appropriate tab, then click the **Fill**, **Line**, or **Text** button at the top of the tab to determine where colour will be applied. The colour of the underline reflects the colour of your selected object.

3. For the Colour tab, select a colour from the colour spectrum or sliders depending on colour mode selected.

   - or -

   ▢ ▦ ▾ For the Swatches tab, select a colour swatch from the **Publication palette** (commonly used colours and those previously applied to your publication) or a specific themed or standard **Palette** (supplied preset swatches).

Alternatively, use **Format>Fill** to apply colour via a dialog.

Using the **Colours** toolbar, you can reapply the last applied fill, line, or text colour and also predefine these colours for future objects. By default, the toolbar is always in view thus aiding design productivity.

To apply the last applied solid colour:

1. Select the object(s) or highlight a range of text.

2. 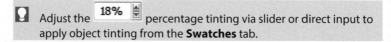 On the **Colours** toolbar, select the **Fill**, **Line**, or **Text** button.

To predefine colours for future objects:

*   With no objects selected, click the down arrow on the toolbar's **Fill**, **Line**, or **Text** buttons and choose a colour from the menu, This is equivalent to using the Colour or Swatches tab.

To change a solid colour's shade/tint (lightness):

1. Select the object and set the correct Fill, Line or Text button in the **Colour** tab.

2. From the Colour mode drop-down list, select **Tinting**.

3. Drag the Shade/Tint slider to the left or right to darken or lighten your starting colour, respectively. You can also enter a value between -100 and 100 in the box. Entering 0 in the input box reverts to the original colour.

> Adjust the **18%** percentage tinting via slider or direct input to apply object tinting from the **Swatches** tab.

PagePlus automatically adds used colours to the **Publication Palette** in the Swatches tab.

To change the current palette:

- On the **Swatches** tab, click the 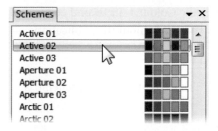 **Palette** button to view and adopt colours from a **Standard RGB**, **Standard CMYK**, or selection of themed palettes. Colours can be added, edited, or deleted from the Publication Palette but not from other palettes.

Using colour schemes

In PagePlus, a **colour scheme** is a cluster of eleven complementary colours (of which **five** are mainly used) that you can apply to specific elements in one or more publications. The **Schemes** tab displays preset schemes (displaying the five main colours) which can be selected at any point during the design process.

Each publication can have just one colour scheme at a time; the current scheme is highlighted in the **Schemes** tab. You can easily switch schemes, modify scheme colours and create custom schemes. Colour schemes are saved globally, so the full set of schemes is always available.

How colour schemes work

Colour schemes in PagePlus work much like a paint-by-numbers system, where various regions of a layout are coded with numbers, and a specific colour is assigned (by number) to each region. For example, imagine a line drawing coded with the numbers 1 through 5. To fill it in, you'd use paint from jars also numbered 1 through 5. Swapping different colours into the paint jars, while keeping the numbers on the drawing the same, would produce quite a different painting.

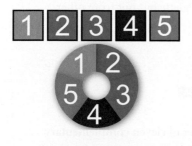

In PagePlus, the "paint jars" are numbers you can assign to objects in your publication. They're known as "Scheme Colour 1," "Scheme Colour 2," and so on. When you apply Scheme Colour 1 to an object, it's like saying, "Put the colour from jar number 1 here."

The **Schemes** tab shows the various available schemes, each with a different set of five colours in the five "jars." Whichever named colour scheme you select, that scheme's first colour (as shown in its sample) will appear in regions defined as Scheme Colour 1, its second colour will map to Scheme Colour 2, and so on throughout the publication.

To select a colour scheme:

1. Click the **Schemes** tab. The currently assigned scheme is highlighted in the list.

   By default, the Schemes tab is collapsed at the bottom right of the workspace.

2. Click a different colour scheme sample. Objects in the publication that have been assigned one of the colour scheme numbers are updated with the corresponding colour from the new scheme.

You can repeat this selection process indefinitely. When you save a publication, its current colour scheme is saved along with the publication.

Applying scheme colours to objects

When you create publications from pre-defined **design templates** (see p. 15), you can choose the starting colour scheme that you want to adopt; you can always change it later from the **Schemes** tab. This flexibility creates endless possibilities for the look and feel of your publication! However, if you then create new elements in your schemed publication, or start a publication from scratch, how can you extend the current colour scheme to the new objects? Although you'll need to spend some time working out which colour combinations look best, the mechanics of the process are simple. Recalling the paint-by-numbers example above, all you need to do is assign one of the current scheme colour numbers to an object's line and/or fill.

To assign a scheme colour to an object:

1. On the **Swatches** tab, from the **Publications Palette** flyout, select **Scheme Colours**.

The palette displays only scheme colours.

2. Select the object and choose a ▬ **Fill**, ▭ **Line**, or ▲ **Text** button at the top of the **Swatches** tab depending on the desired effect.

3. Click on the scheme colour that you want to apply to the fill, line, or text.

If an object's fill uses a scheme colour, the corresponding sample in **Swatches** tab will be highlighted whenever the object is selected.

PagePlus also allows you to modify any existing colour scheme and create your own scheme from a colour spread. See PagePlus Help for more information.

Gradient and bitmap fills

Gradient fills provide a gradation or spectrum of colours spreading between two or more points on an object. A gradient fill has an editable path with handles that mark the origin of each of these key colours. A bitmap fill uses a named bitmap—often a material, pattern, or background image—to fill an object.

Linear   *Elliptical*   *Conical*   *Bitmap*

You can apply preset gradient and bitmap fills from the Swatches tab to the fill or outline of a **shape** or **text frame**. **Table cells** as well as **artistic**, **frame**, and table text can also take a gradient or bitmap fill.

The fill's path on an object's fill or line can also be varied for different effects (see PagePlus Help).

Nulla quis nibh. Proin
ac pede vel ligula
facilisis gravida.
Phasellus purus. Etiam
sapien. Duis diam
iaculis ut, vehicula

Lorem ipsum

Applying a gradient or bitmap fill

There are several ways to apply a gradient or bitmap fill: using the **Swatches** tab, the **Fill Tool**, or the **Fill** dialog.

PagePlus can also produce automatic gradient fills based on applied solid colours—giving you an almost unlimited number of gradient fill choices.

The easiest way to apply a gradient or bitmap fill is to use one of a range of pre-supplied swatch thumbnails in the Swatches tab's **Gradient** or **Bitmap** palettes. The **Fill Tool** and a Fill dialog are alternative methods for creating gradient fills.

To apply an automatic gradient:

1. Select an object with a **solid colour applied** to its fill and/or outline (see p. 149).

2. � Display the Swatches tab and ensure either **Fill** or **Line** is selected (for an object's fill or outline, respectively). Note that the colour of the underline reflects the colour of your selected object.

3. ▪ ▾ From the **Gradient** button's drop-down list, select the **Automatic** category.

   The palette displays a range of gradients based on the solid colour already applied to the fill or line.

4. Click a swatch for the fill you want to apply.

To apply a preset gradient or bitmap fill using the Swatches tab:

1. ▪ ▫ Display the Swatches tab and ensure either **Fill** or **Line** is selected (for an object's fill or outline, respectively). Note that the colour of the underline reflects the colour of your selected object.

2. ▪ ▾ For gradient fills, select a gradient category, e.g. Linear, Elliptical, etc., from the **Gradient** button's drop-down list.
   - or -

   ▨ ▾ For bitmap fills, select a drop-down list category from the **Bitmap** button.

3. Select the object(s), and then click the appropriate gallery swatch for the fill you want to apply.
   - or -

   Drag a gallery swatch onto any object (it doesn't need to be selected) and release the mouse button. This will affect the object's Fill colour but not its Line colour.

4. If needed, adjust the fill's **Tint** at the bottom of the tab with the tab slider or set a percentage value in the input box.

🖎 Applying different transparency effects (using the **Transparency** tab) won't alter the object's fill settings as such, but may significantly alter a fill's actual appearance.

To apply a gradient fill with the Fill Tool:

1. Select an object.

2. Click the  **Fill Tool** on the **Attributes** toolbar.

3. Display the Swatches tab and ensure either **Fill** or **Line** is selected (for an object's fill or outline, respectively).

4. Click and drag on the object to define the fill path. The object takes a simple Linear fill, grading from the object's current colour to monochrome white.

> If the object is white already (or has no fill), grading is from white to black.

To modify a gradient using the context toolbar:

1. With the object selected, click the **Fill Tool** on the **Attributes** toolbar.

2. On the context toolbar:

    *   Choose the fill type from the drop-down list. (You can also apply a **Solid** or **None** fill type.)

    *   From the **Start Colour** drop-down list, select a colour or click **More Colours** to display the **Colour Selector** dialog.

You can also apply an **End Colour** in the same way.
- or -

For **Three** or **Four Colour** only, select an object's fill
handle and select a colour from the ![icon] **Fill Colour** drop-
down list.

Alternatively, a dialog can be used to add or subtract **key colours** from
the gradient, apply different key colours to individual handles, or vary
the overall shading of the effect applied to the object.

To apply or edit a gradient or bitmap fill using a dialog:

1.   ![icon] ![icon] Display the Swatches tab and ensure either **Fill** or
     Line is selected (for an object's fill or outline, respectively).

2.   ![icon] ![icon] Click the **Fill Tool** on the **Attributes** toolbar and
     then, on the context toolbar, click **Edit Fill**.

Editing the fill path

When you select a fillable object, the **Fill Tool** becomes available (otherwise it's greyed out). When you select the Fill Tool, if the object uses a **gradient fill**, you'll see the **fill path** displayed as a line, with handles marking where the spectrum between each key colour begins and ends. Adjusting the handle positions determines the actual spread of colours between handles. You can also edit a gradient fill by adding, deleting, or changing key colours.

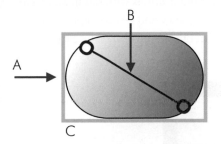

(**A**) *Linear Fill based on key colours,* (**B**) *Path,* (**C**) *Effect on Object*

To adjust the gradient fill path on a selected object:

1. Display the Swatches tab and ensure either **Fill** or **Line** is selected (for an object's fill or outline, respectively).

2. Click the **Fill Tool** on the **Attributes** toolbar. The fill path appears on the object's fill or outline.

3. Use the **Fill Tool** to drag the start and end path handles, or click on the object for a new start handle and drag out a new fill path. The gradient starts where you place the start handle, and ends where you place the end handle.

Each gradient fill type has a characteristic path. For example, Linear fills have single-line paths, while Radial fills have a two-line path so you can adjust the fill's extent in two directions away from the centre.

If the object uses a **bitmap fill**, you'll see the fill path displayed as two lines joined at a centre point. Handles mark the fill's centre and edges.

Working with transparency

Transparency effects are great for highlights, shading and shadows, and simulating "rendered" realism. They can make the critical difference between flat-looking publications and publications with depth and snap. PagePlus fully supports variable transparency and lets you apply solid, gradient, or bitmap transparency to an object's fill or outline easily.

Transparencies work rather like fills that use "disappearing ink" instead of colour. The more transparency in a particular spot, the more "disappearing" takes place there, and the more the object(s) underneath show through. Just as a **gradient fill** can vary from light to dark, a transparency can vary from more to less, i.e. from clear to opaque:

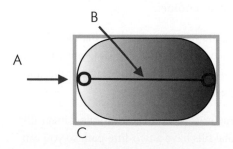

(A) Linear Transparency, (B) Path, (C) Effect on Object

Transparency types available in the Transparency tab are as follows:

- **Solid** transparency distributes the transparency uniformly.

- **Gradient** transparencies include linear, elliptical, and conical effects, ranging from clear to opaque.

- **Bitmap** transparencies include categorized texture maps based on the Swatches tab's selection of bitmaps.

Applying transparency

You can apply transparency to **shapes**, **text frames**, table cells, and to any **artistic**, **frame**, and table text.

To apply transparency with Transparency tab:

1. With your object selected, display the Transparency tab and ensure either **Fill** or **Line** is selected (for an object's fill or outline, respectively).

2. For solid transparency, select the ☐ **Solid** button and pick a thumbnail from the solid transparency gallery.
    - or -

    For gradient transparency, choose the ◼ **Gradient** button and pick your thumbnail.
    - or -

    For bitmap transparency, choose the ▦ ▾ **Bitmap** button and pick a thumbnail from a range of categories.

    The transparency is applied to the object's fill or outline.

3. Alternatively, drag the desired thumbnail from the gallery to an object, and release the mouse button.

To apply gradient transparency with the Transparency Tool:

1. Select the object and set the Transparency tab's Fill/Line swatch as before.

2. Click the ⚲ **Transparency Tool** on the **Attributes** toolbar.

3. Drag your cursor across the object and release the mouse button. The object takes a simple Linear transparency, grading from 100% opacity to 0% opacity (fully transparent).

Editing transparency

Once you've applied a gradient transparency, you can adjust or replace its **path** on the object, and the **level** of transparency along the path. You can even create more complex transparency effects by adding extra handles to the path by clicking and assigning different levels to each handle.

To adjust the transparency path:

- Use the ⚲ **Transparency Tool** to drag individual handles, or click on the object for a new start handle and drag out a new transparency path. The effect starts where you place the start handle, and ends where you place the end handle. For bitmap transparencies, the path determines the centre and two edges of the effect.

Editing a **gradient transparency** path is similar to editing a comparable **fill path**. Adding a level of transparency means varying the transparency gradient by introducing a new **handle** and assigning it a particular value. For transparencies with multiple handles, each handle has its own value, comparable to a key colour in a gradient fill. Note that you cannot alter the values in a bitmap transparency.

To edit a gradient transparency directly:

1. Select the object and set the Transparency tab's **Fill/Line** swatch as before.

2. Click the Ⴘ **Transparency Tool** on the **Attributes** toolbar. The object's transparency path appears on the fill or line, with start and end handles.

3. To **add** a transparency handle, drag from any **solid transparency** sample in the Transparency tab to the point on the path where you want to add the handle.

    The higher the percentage value assigned to a transparency handle, the more transparent the effect at that point. Note: The hue of the colour doesn't matter, only its percentage value—so it's much easier just to choose from the set of gallery thumbnails.

4. To **change** the transparency value of any existing handle, including the start and end handles, select the handle and click on a new thumbnail in the Transparency tab's Solid transparency gallery (you can also drag your chosen thumbnail onto the selected handle).

5. To **move** a handle you've added, simply drag it to a new position along the transparency path.

6. To **delete** a handle you've added, select it and press the **Delete** key.

Composite transparency

An individual object can take a specific transparency setting. In addition, when multiple objects are **grouped**, the group can also be given a **composite transparency**, affecting all group objects to the same extent.

The example on the right has composite transparency applied, while the example on the left does not.

To apply composite transparency:

1. Select a *group*.

2. Apply transparency from the **Transparency** tab.

3. From the context toolbar, enable **Composite Transparency**.

Understanding blend modes

You can think of **blend modes** as different rules for putting overlaying pixels together to create a resulting colour. Note that blend modes work in relation to the colours of the objects themselves (shapes, lines, etc).

They are used for **creative effects** on overlapping objects, where colours blend on top of one another. Blend modes can be applied to both a top object's line and fill colour. You can adjust the blend mode of an existing object on your page, or you can set the blend mode before creating a line, shape, etc.

Yellow flower on page background

The same flower with an **Exclusion** *blend mode applied*

To apply a blend mode to an existing object:

1. Select an existing object on your page.

2. On the **Colour tab**, choose a blend mode from the **Blend Mode** drop-down list.

To apply a blend mode to a new line or shape:

1. Select the line or shape tool you want to use, and set its appropriate settings—width, colour, etc.

2. On the **Colour** tab, choose a blend mode from the **Blend Mode** drop-down list.

3. Create your line or shape on your page.

> The **On-page Colour** of your page is also affected by blend modes applied to objects. This may not be immediately clear as, by default, the On-page Colour of PagePlus X7 publications is set to transparent and will therefore show no change. For more information on setting an On-page Colour, see **Setting individual page properties** in PagePlus Help.

When multiple objects are grouped, the group can be given a **composite blend mode**, which complements any blend mode applied to objects prior to being grouped. The composite blend is applied to the group after objects have been blended.

To apply a composite blend mode:

1. Select a group.

2. From the Group context toolbar, select a blend mode from the drop-down list.

Blend modes applied to overlapping objects may produce unwanted blending on underlying objects; the blending between overlapping objects within the group might be all that is required. This can be overcome by using **isolated blending**.

To apply isolated blending:

1. Select the grouped object containing blending.

2. From the context toolbar, enable **Isolated Blending**.

For a complete list of blend modes, with supporting examples, please see the topic **Understanding blend modes** in PagePlus help.

Publishing and Sharing

12

Preflight check

Preflight is an essential process to ensure that your PagePlus output, whether PDF, HTML or eBook, is published as intended. You can run a preflight check at any time during your design process to fix issues as they occur. In addition, when a problem is encountered on publishing, the preflight check will report the problem in the **Preflight** tab automatically, allowing you to check, locate, and fix the problem.

Our example shows a sample of the warnings which you may encounter if publishing a publication as a PDF:

It is not mandatory to resolve the warnings, in some cases PagePlus will work around the problem automatically on publishing. However, by resolving the warnings, your final publication should provide users with a better experience when accessing your PDF, HTML files, or eBook.

Manual preflight check

Checking your publication as you design is particularly useful when
working toward a specific output which must comply with a rigid layout
and style, such as HTML or eBook. You can then resolve problems as
they arise, saving you time when you finally come to publish your
publication.

To run a manual Preflight check:

1. Select **Tabs>Preflight Tab** from the **View** menu.

2. In the **Preflight** tab's drop-down list, select the final publication
    type.

3. Click ☑ **Check** to run the preflight check. Any warnings will
    be listed in the **Preflight** tab.

To resolve problems listed in the Preflight check:

1. Select a warning from the list.

    A brief explanation of the warning displays at the bottom of the
    Preflight tab.

2. (Optional) Click 🗐 **Help** to get immediate help on how to
    resolve your publishing problem.

3. Click 🔍 **Locate** to automatically select the problem object.

4. Modify the object as appropriate.

    - or -

    Click 📋 **Fix** to resolve the publishing problem automatically (not valid for all warnings).

5. (Optional) Click 📋 **Check** to run the preflight check again.

This is useful once you've resolved a problem and you need to verify your fix before republishing.

Automated preflight check

PagePlus will automatically run a check of your publication when you publish as PDF, HTML, or eBook. This automated check is more comprehensive than the manual check **discussed above** as it also covers the options set in the Publish as dialogs. If there are any problems with the publication, the **Preflight** tab will automatically open, displaying a list of issues.

A warning dialog will also display, asking whether you wish to proceed with the export and ignore the listed problems. Click **Yes** to continue with publication or **No** to work through the issues before publishing.

To resolve the listed problems, follow the steps listed.

Interactive Print/PDF Preview

The **Print/PDF Preview** mode changes the screen view to display your page layout without frames, guides, rulers, and other screen items. Supporting toolbars allow for a comprehensive and interactive preview of your publication pages before **printing** or **publishing as PDF**.

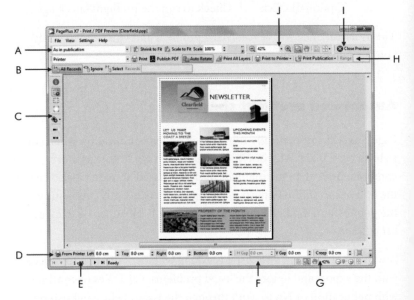

(A) Imposition toolbar, (B) Mail and Photo Merge toolbar (hidden by default), (C) Page Marks toolbar, (D) Margins toolbar, (E) Page Navigation tools, (F) Hintline toolbar, (G) View tools, (H) Printer toolbar, (I) Close toolbar, (J) View toolbar (hidden by default).

The Preview is interactive—its main feature is to provide dynamic **print-time imposition**. Put simply, this allows you to create folded books, booklets, and more, **at the printing/publication stage** from unfolded basic publication setups.

To preview the page:

1. Click  **Print/PDF Preview** on the **Standard** toolbar.

    In Print/PDF Preview, your first printer sheet is displayed according to your printer's setup.

2. (Optional) Choose an installed printer from the **Printer** toolbar's drop-down list.

3. (Optional) Adjust printer margins from the **Margins** toolbar.

4. Review your publication using the page navigation controls at the bottom of your workspace.

To print via Printer toolbar:

1. Choose which page to print via the toolbar's **Print Publication** drop-down list. For 'Print Specific Pages', type page number(s) into the **Range** box.

2. Select 🖶 **Print**.

The standard **Print** dialog is then displayed, where settings are carried over from Preview mode (see **Printing basics** on p. 175).

To publish as PDF via Printer toolbar:

*   Select 📄 **Publish PDF**.

The standard **Publish PDF** dialog is then displayed (see **Publishing PDF files** on p. 177).

To cancel Preview mode:

*   Select ❌ **Close Preview** from the top of your workspace (or click the window's ❌ **Close** button).

Document imposition in Preview mode

During preview, you can enable imposition of your document, choosing a mode suited to your intended final publication (book, booklet, etc.). Each mode displays different toolbar options on the context-sensitive **Imposition** toolbar. Document imposition is not limited to desktop printing—it can also be used when creating a press-ready PDF for professional printing.

To choose an imposition mode:

- From the **Imposition** toolbar, select an option from the **Imposition Mode** drop-down list.

As in publication
As in publication
Tiled
Print as Thumbnails
Side Fold Book
Side Fold Booklet
Top Fold Book
Top Fold Booklet
N-up
Step & Repeat

Shrink to Fit   Scale to Fit   Scale 100%   Fit Ma

Printing books and booklets

To produce double-sided sheets, click 🖶 **Print** and use the Print dialog's Double-sided Printing or Manual Duplex options (under **More Options**). Ensure your printer is setup for double-sided printing or run sheets through twice, printing first the front and then the back of the sheet (reverse top and bottom between runs). The sheets can then be collated and bound at their centre to produce a booklet, with all the pages in the correct sequence.

Printing basics

Printing your publication to a desktop printer is one of the more likely
operations you'll be performing in PagePlus. The easy-to-use Print
dialog presents the most commonly used options to you, with a
navigable "live" Preview window to check your print output.

The dialog also supports additional printing options via the **More
Options** button including **Double-sided Printing**, **Mail Merge**,
Rasterize, and many other useful printing options. One particular
option, called **Layout** (p. 174), allows for print-time imposition of your
publication—simply create a booklet or other folded publication at the
print stage.

Here we'll cover what you need to know for basic desktop printer
output. If you're working with a service bureau or professional printer
and need to provide PDF output, see **Exporting PDF files** (p. 177).

To set up your printer or begin printing:

1. (Optional) To print selected text or objects, make your selection on the page.

2. Click 🖶 **Print** on the **Standard** toolbar.

   The **Print** dialog appears.

To set your printing options:

1. Select a currently installed printer from the **Printer** drop-down list. If necessary, click the **Properties** button to set up the printer for the correct page size, etc.

2. Select a printer profile from the **Profile** drop-down list. You can just use **Current Settings** or choose a previously saved custom profile (.ppr) based on a combination of dialog settings; **Browse** lets you navigate to any .ppr file on your computer. To save current settings, click the **Save As** button, and provide a unique profile name. The profile is added to the drop-down list.

   If you modify any profile settings, an asterisk appears next to the profile name.

3. Select the number of copies to print, and optionally instruct the printer to **Collate** them.

4. Select the print **Range** to be printed, e.g. the Entire Publication, Current Page, Current Selection (if selected text or objects in step 1), or range of pages. For specific pages or a range of pages, enter "1,3,5" or "2-5", or enter any combination of the two.

   Whichever option you've chosen, the **Include** drop-down list lets you export all sheets in the range, or just odd or even sheets, with the option of printing in **Reverse** order.

5. Set a percentage **Scale** which will enlarge or shrink your print output (both page and contents). A 100% scale factor creates a full size print output. Alternatively, from the adjacent drop-down list, choose **Shrink to Fit** to reduce your publication's page size to the printer sheet size or **Scale to Fit** to enlarge or reduce the publication page size as required.

6. Keep **Auto Rotate** checked if you want your publication page to automatically rotate your printer's currently set sheet orientation. When you access the Print dialog, if page and sheet sizes do not match, you'll be prompted to adjust your printer sheet orientation automatically (or you can just ignore auto-rotation).

7. Click **Print**.

More print options

Additional print options are available from the Print dialog if you're planning to use **imposition at print time** (see p. 174), use specific PagePlus features which use printing (e.g., **Mail Merge**), **print double-sided**, or generate professional output.

Publishing PDF files

PagePlus can output your publications to PDF (Portable Document Format), a cross-platform WYSIWYG file format developed by Adobe, intended to handle documents in a device- and platform-independent manner.

PDF documents are ideal for both **web-ready** distribution and **professional** printing.

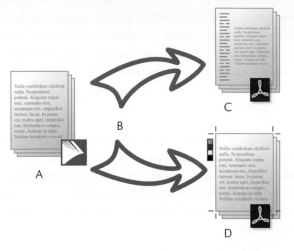

(A) PagePlus Publication, (B) Preflight and Publish, (C) web-ready PDF, (D) Press-ready PDF (professional).

In PagePlus, ready-to-go PDF profiles are available for both uses, making PDF setup less complicated.

Preflight checking

To assist you as you design, you can perform a manual preflight check as you go. On publishing, a preflight check is also run automatically, alerting you to any design problems that would result in sub-optimal published results. See **Preflight check** on p. 169 for more information.

The preflight check also offers solutions to resolve PDF publishing issues.

Publishing to PDF

To publish as a PDF file (using a profile):

1. Click ![icon] **Publish as PDF** on the **Standard** toolbar.

2. Select a profile for screen-ready or professional output from the
    Profile drop-down list.

The dialog updates with the selected profile's new settings. The
Compatibility is set according to the profile and doesn't need
to be changed.

3. Select the **Range** to be published, e.g. the Entire Publication,
    Current Page, or range of pages. For specific pages or a range of
    pages, enter "1,3,5" or "2-5", or enter any combination of the
    two .

4. Set a percentage **Scale** which will enlarge or shrink your
    published output (both page and contents). A 100% scale factor
    creates a full size print output.

5. (Optional) Click **More Options** and make any additional
    settings as required.

6. Click **OK**.

Saving PDF profiles

To save any current combination of your own PDF output settings as a
custom publish profile with a unique name, click the **Save As** button
next to the Publish profile list. Type in a new name and click OK. In a
subsequent session you can recall the profile by selecting its name from
the list.

More PDF options

The dialog also supports additional PDF publishing options via the
More Options button including **Layout**, **Prepress**, and **Colour
Management**.

```
Layout
Prepress
Compression
Colour Management
Fonts
Fills and Transparency
Security
```

Creating a PDF bookmark list

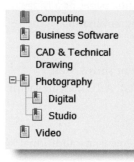

Bookmarks are optional links that
appear in a separate pane of the PDF
reader when a PDF file is displayed.

Typically, a bookmark links to a
specific location such as a section
heading in the publication, but it can
also link to a whole page or specifically
to an **anchor** attached to an object.

To use styles to automatically generate bookmarks:

1. Select **PDF Bookmarks** from the **Insert** menu.

2. In the dialog, click **Automatic**. You'll see a list of all the style
    names available to PagePlus. Check boxes to include text of a
    given style as a heading at a particular level (1 through 6). For
    example, for Heading 1, Heading 2, and Heading 3 at three
    hierarchical levels:

Style	1st	2nd	3rd	4th	5th	6th
Footer	☐	☐	☐	☐	☐	☐
Header	☐	☐	☐	☐	☐	☐
Header an...	☐	☐	☐	☐	☐	☐
Heading	☐	☐	☐	☐	☐	☐
Heading 1	☒	☐	☐	☐	☐	☐
Heading 2	☐	☒	☐	☐	☐	☐
Heading 3	☐	☐	☒	☐	☐	☐
Heading 4	☐	☐	☐	☐	☐	☐

3. Click **OK** to generate bookmarks.

> You can also create your own custom PDF bookmark list. See PagePlus Help for more information.

Unlike hyperlinks, bookmarks also work as actual links within PagePlus publications. You can use the bookmark list as a jumping-off point to any bookmarked entry.

Creating a PDF slideshow

The creation of PDF slideshows takes PagePlus's **PDF publishing** a step further. While a PDF file shows the exact replication of your original project for electronic distribution or printing, the PDF slideshow feature does the same, but with the intention of creating automated multimedia presentations. These can be shared by email and viewed without the need for special presentation software.

To publish a slideshow:

1. Select **Publish As>PDF Slideshow** from the **File** menu.

2. In the **Publish PDF slideshow** dialog, from the **Slideshow** options (click ⊙ **More Options**, if needed):

    *   Select a default **Transition** type for all slides, e.g. Blinds, Wipe, or Dissolve.

        An individual slide can override this setting with its own transition setting.

    *   Check **Manual Advance** if you don't want your slideshow to display slides one by one automatically— slides will be progressed manually by mouse-click or by pressing the space bar.

        - or -

        For automatic slideshows, choose a **Duration**, i.e. the number of seconds each slide will remain on screen.

    *   When your slideshow reaches the last page you can **Loop slideshow** continuously or **Return to normal view** to exit the slideshow.

    *   For accompanying music, click **Browse** to navigate to and select an audio file.

3. To set individual slide properties and rearrange the playback order of existing slides, click **Configure Slides**.

4. Click **OK**.

5. In the dialog, save your named PDF file to a chosen location. If **Preview PDF file in Acrobat** was checked, your slideshow will start to run automatically.

Multi-section slides

One strength of the slideshow feature comes from the ability to make "multi-section" slide variants based on a single PagePlus page (this is done using page layers). Multi-section slides allow you to build up an image in sections; display multiple images and text objects sequentially on the same page; show and hide page elements; and so on.

See PagePlus Help for more information.

Publishing as eBooks

The emergence of eBooks in recent years offers not just the traditional book publishers an opportunity to explore new electronic book markets, but also provides the writer with the ability to publish their own eBooks.

In PagePlus, you can be your own publisher and create eBooks in both **ePub** and **mobi** formats. Like **publishing to PDF** and HTML, the process of eBook publishing is straightforward, with the added benefit of manual and automatic **preflight checking** to ensure your file conforms to eBook standards.

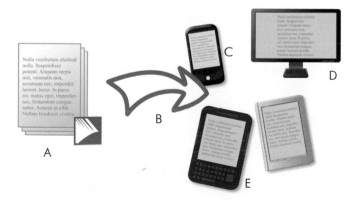

(A) PagePlus Publication, (B) Preflight and Publish, (C) Smart phone, (D) Computer, (E) Kindle/ePub readers.

Design tips and tricks

If you plan to create eBooks effortlessly there are several useful do's and don'ts that you should bear in mind during eBook design.

When designing eBooks, do:

- Pre-plan your eBook's design in advance of publishing.

- Avoid using design templates; instead start from scratch.

- Keep your story contained within text frames.

- Use pre-supplied heading text styles in your story.

- Create a single TOC.

- Create a **cover for your eBook** as a picture (p. 187).

Conversely, don't:

- Place any object (picture, artistic, header/footer text, etc.) outside the main text frame.

- **Anchor** floating objects to your text frame. Anchored inline objects are acceptable.

- Create excessively long chapters (<300k is recommended).

> For more help about optimizing **Amazon Kindle publishing**, see the **Amazon Kindle Publishing Guidelines**.

Publishing

Two approaches can be taken depending on which devices you intend to publish for, i.e. to ePub or Kindle. Both publishing processes are similar, except that they create different file formats (i.e., *.epub and *.mobi, respectively). Kindle publishing additionally requires the KindleGen program to be installed on your computer.

To publish an eBook for ePub devices:

1. Choose **Publish As>** from the **File** menu and select **eBook** from the submenu.

2. From the dialog's Document Info menu, add metadata, an ID, and a **pre-designed eBook cover** (if needed).

3. With the Output menu item selected, control how tables, lists, and pictures are to be exported.

4. With the Styles menu item selected, you can control how your publication's currently used **text styles** affect your eBook after publishing. Select a text style from the list, then select an **Action for this style**.

5. Click **OK**.

6. In the **Publish eBook** dialog, navigate to the location where you wish to publish your eBook, then enter a file name in the **File name** box. Keep the **Save as type** drop-down list set to "ePub files (*.epub)".

7. Click **Save**.

To publish an eBook for Kindle:

1. Install the KindleGen program, downloadable from **Amazon Kindle publishing**.

2. Follow the procedure as for ePub devices above.

3. In the dialog's Output menu, under the Kindle section, click **Browse** to navigate to (and select) the kindlegen.exe file from the installed folder above and click **Open**.

4. Click **OK**.

5. From the **Publish eBook** dialog, navigate to a folder, choose a filename, and change the **Save as type** drop-down list to "Kindle files (*.mobi)".

6. Click **Save**.

If you checked **Show document after publication**, the ePub book will launch in its associated reader.

> If you've not already downloaded KindleGen, click **Download KindleGen from Amazon**. This takes you directly to the **Amazon Kindle publishing** website.

Previewing and validating Kindle books

Any kindle book (*.mobi) you create can be previewed on your computer before transferring it to your Kindle device (or uploading to Amazon).

There are a variety of devices which allow you to preview your kindle book on your computer, however, if you install Kindle Previewer software (available from **Amazon Kindle publishing**), you can also use this as a way to validate the content formatting of your book to ensure it will display correctly on the entire range of Kindle devices and applications.

Displaying your eBook

Once you've published your eBook you'll want to make it available to a physical device as soon as possible. Typical ways that your eBook can be read, include:

*   Via **computer**: Install **Adobe Digital Editions** software to view your ePub document. Similarly, **Kindle Previewer** software is the choice for Kindle files.

- Via **Kindle/Android phone**: Transfer your published *.mobi file by copying to your device via your USB port. Alternatively, you can send your file via email directly to your device.

- Via **ePub physical device/Android phone**: Like Kindle devices, you can transfer your *.epub file to your device via USB.

Setting output formats and alternate text for individual objects

Like in HTML publishing, you can select an object and force it to be converted to a picture on publishing. You would do this to ensure conformance to eBook standards, perhaps after a failed **preflight check**.

Creating a book cover

You can include a picture when you export your publication which will act as a front cover for your eBook. The picture will need to be created before you can fully complete the eBook exporting process.

Your cover can be designed in several ways which may include:

- Designing a cover using graphics, photos, artistic text and assets within a PagePlus publication and then exporting the page (or specific objects) as a picture. See **Exporting as a picture** on p. 188 for details.

If you intend on exporting your eBook as a *.mobi (for Kindle), you can design your cover on the first page of your publication and it will automatically be output as your eBook cover. If you design using floating objects (not placed in a text frame), this will prevent them appearing within the body of the eBook. Note: this method of cover design will display errors during preflight. See **Preflight check** on p. 169 and eBook publishing warnings in PagePlus Help for more information.

- Using a separate photo editing or illustration program (e.g., Serif PhotoPlus or DrawPlus) and then exporting to a picture.

- Scanning your design or taking a screenshot of a design displayed on your screen.

Whichever method you choose, you should take into consideration the following factors:

- The picture should be exported as a **GIF**, **PNG**, **JPG**, or **SVG**, at no more than **96 dpi**.

- The exported picture's file size should not exceed **128 KB**. Check your exported file size in Windows Explorer.

- The picture will scale to fit to the device's screen or application window size you are using to view the eBook.

Exporting as a picture

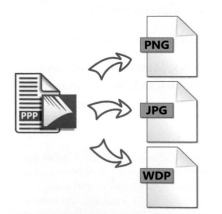

The Export as Picture feature helps reduce file sizes and download times while exporting the **individual page**, **all pages**, selected area, or just the selected object(s). You can also see how your picture will look (and how much space it will take up) before you save it!

For visual comparison, a multi-window display provides side-by-side WYSIWYG previews to compare different formats (below), or the same format using differing settings.

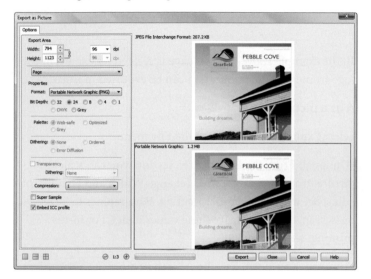

A page export showing Dual Preview window.

A selected object export showing Quad Preview window (window only).

Several common reasons to export as picture include:

- Creating a first-page graphic of your publication for book promotion or design previews.

- Creating an eBook cover.

- Exporting an object (or selection of objects) for use in website design.

- In the example above, a cover page is created on export, or the logo from the same publication can be exported in isolation.

To export as a picture:

1. Select **Export as Picture** from the **File** menu.

2. (Optional) From the Export Area section, you can scale the picture to a new size if desired (change **Width** and **Height**), or adjust the **dpi** (dots per inch) setting. For graphics to be used on-screen, it's best to leave these values intact. For hi-res printing, set a dpi of 300.

3. From the drop-down list, choose if the export can be based on the whole **Page**, **All Pages**, **Selected Area**, or **Selected Objects**. The last two options only show if a selection is made previously.

4. From the Properties section, select the intended graphics file format from the **Format** drop-down list. The remaining box area will display different options depending on your chosen graphics format. Change settings as appropriate to the file format selected (see DrawPlus Help for more information).

5. Click **Export**. If you click **Close**, PagePlus remembers your preferred format and settings.

6. From the Export as Picture dialog, navigate to a folder of your choice, enter a File name, then click **Save**.

Additional Information

13

Contacting Serif

Help with your Product

On the web

Com **unity** **Plus**   **community.serif.com**
Get answers and ask questions in the Serif
community! Type 'PagePlus X7' to filter
PagePlus only articles.

Serif Support   **www.serif.com/support**
For Serif Account and Customer Service
information.

Additional Serif information

On the web	
Serif website	**www.serif.com**
Main office	
Address	The Software Centre, PO Box 2000 Nottingham, NG11 7GW, UK
Phone	(0115) 914 2000
Phone (Registration)	(0800) 376 1989 +44 800 376 1989 800-794-6876 (US, Canada)
Phone (Sales)	(0800) 376 7070 +44 800 376 7070 800-489-6703 (US, Canada)
Customer Service	0845 345 6770 800-489-6720 (US, Canada)
Fax	(0115) 914 2020

Credits

This User Guide, and the software described in it, is furnished under an end user License Agreement, which is included with the product. The agreement specifies the permitted and prohibited uses.

Trademarks

Serif is a registered trademark of Serif (Europe) Ltd.

PagePlus is a registered trademark of Serif (Europe) Ltd.

All Serif product names are trademarks of Serif (Europe) Ltd.

Microsoft, Windows, and the Windows logo are registered trademarks of Microsoft Corporation. All other trademarks acknowledged.

Windows Vista and the Windows Vista Start button are trademarks or registered trademarks of Microsoft Corporation in the United States and/or other countries.

Kindle, the AmazonKindle logo, and Whispersync are trademarks of Amazon.com, Inc. or its affiliates.

Nook is a trademark of Barnes & Noble, Inc.

Copyrights

Index

14